Praise for *We Are*

'Emotional pain needs to be named, understood and
medicalised, suppressed or labelled. These poems, written from
the heart, are beacons of courage for those in search of liberation.'
*Professor Emmy van Deurzen, philosopher, existential therapist
and author*

'Poetry has always been an important part of the emotional
toolkit. In writing it, we can express anguish or find a way through
confusion; in reading it, we can find comfort for our own distress
and recognise that others have experienced the same things we have.
The poems in this collection come from the extremes of emotion.
A good poem always costs you something to write; in sharing a
moment of crisis or revelation, the poet is naked and vulnerable.
These pieces are reports from the front line. In reading them and
learning from them, you show solidarity with the writers.'
Jo Bell, poet

'What a rollercoaster of emotions! These are poems of truth, pain
and power reclaimed. I salute the poets for their courage.'
Deborah Alma, Emergency Poet and founder of the Poetry Pharmacy

'These are the voices of rebel souls, truth tellers, the defiant and
the righteous. Each poem is threaded through with tragedy, but
they are not tragic. I laughed out loud, sang songs of victory and
cried full moons as these poets' words went deep into my heart.
Some hit home, and others pull you in, compelling you to lean in
and show solidarity. This book is rich, full and will take you on a
journey from which there is no turning back. You will, I know, be
transformed forever. To the beautiful, shining stars in this book, I
say thank you.'
*Dr Akima Thomas OBE, founder and clinical director, Women
and Girls Network*

'*We Are the Change Makers*, with its many fine and moving poems, powerfully tells of the harm that the DSM inflicts on so many people. It is also a testament to the power of poetry to serve as a call to action. At the conclusion of this book, every reader will understand that striving to "Drop the Disorder" is a worthy goal.'
Robert Whitaker, journalist and author, founder of madinamerica. com

'A courageous and inspiring poetry collection on a really important subject.'
Johann Hari, journalist and writer

We Are the Change-Makers

*Poems supporting
Drop the Disorder!*

edited by
Jo Watson

First published 2020

PCCS Books Ltd
Wyastone Business Park
Wyastone Leys
Monmouth
NP25 3SR
UK

Tel +44 (0)1600 891509
contact@pccs-books.co.uk
www.pccs-books.co.uk

We Are the Change-Makers: poems supporting Drop the Disorder!

British Library Cataloguing in Publication Data.
A catalogue record for this book is available from the British Library

ISBNs
paperback – 978 1 910919 64 4
epub – 978 1 910919 66 8

Cover design by Jason Anscomb
Printed in the UK by TJ Books Limited, Padstow

Contents

Dedication

For Pat, my very favourite change-maker.

Acknowledgements

Thank you PCCS Books, for yet again supporting this urgent discussion in such a proactive way – especially Commissioning Editor Catherine Jackson for her endless supply of belief and encouragement.

And thank you to all the contributors, who have shared their work here in the spirit of solidarity with an unwavering commitment to and passion for change.

This book was named with you all in mind.

'The moment of change is the only poem.'
Adrienne Rich, from 'The Will to Change', in *The Will to Change: Poems 1968-1970* (W.W. Norton & Co, 1971)

'... poetry is the perfect medium to tell difficult and marginalised stories... It brings our rational side together with our emotions and makes us whole once again, ready to resist and defy.'
Choman Hardi, from 'Poetry's Power to Speak the Unspeakable: the Kurdish story', *LSE Women, Peace and Security* (https://blogs.lse.ac.uk/wps)

'A poet's work is to name the unnameable, to point at frauds, to take sides, start arguments, shape the world and stop it from going to sleep.'
Salman Rushdie, *The Independent*, 18 February, 1989

'Poetry is the way we help give name to the nameless so it can be thought. The farthest horizons of our hopes and fears are cobbled by our poems, carved from the rock experiences of our daily lives.'
Audre Lorde, from 'Poetry is Not A Luxury', in *Sister Outsider: Essays and Speeches* (Ten Speed Press, 1984)

'I do not believe in silence.'
Clare Shaw, from *Head On* (Bloodaxe, 2012)

Introduction

'Poetry is the lifeblood of rebellion, revolution, and the raising of consciousness.'
Alice Walker

All of the contributors in this book want change. They want to see an end to the pathologising of people's pain, an end to the labelling, the locking up, the electro-shock, the drugging at first response, the individualising and the scapegoating.

They want something different. Something better. Something more humane.

And so do I.

For the last four years, Lucy Johnstone and I, accompanied by our ally Nollaig McSweeney, have taken the 'Drop the Disorder!' message around the UK in an event called 'A Disorder for Everyone', or AD4E.

The day is so named because of our belief that Western psychiatry has pathologised understandable human responses and experiences to such an extent that we all fit one DSM[1] category or another. There really is a disorder for everyone!

The response to the event has been extremely encouraging. We've witnessed a genuine and growing desire for a movement away from the culture of diagnosis and disorder. We've been heartened by the willingness of people to get actively involved in their own ways in bringing about change. The Drop the Disorder! Facebook group that we set up at around the same time as the first event now has more than 12,000 members, and the *Drop the Disorder!* book (Watson, 2019) has been a best-seller since its publication in September 2019.

---

1. The DSM is *The Diagnostic and Statistical Manual of Mental Disorders*, now in its fifth edition (*DSM-5*). This is the compendium of diagnostic categories used by psychiatrists to identify, describe and treat (with drugs) people's experience of emotional distress worldwide. It is published by the American Psychiatric Association.

1

There definitely seems to be an appetite to join this debate.

The AD4E events challenge the dominant narrative that imposes scientifically invalid diagnostic explanations on people's experiences of emotional distress. They explore a range of alternative, socially responsive, trauma-informed, strengths-based ways of responding.

We have had many people join us from a variety of backgrounds to contribute to the day, which has meant that each event, in each city, has had its own particular flavour. However, one consistent feature of the AD4E experience, ever since the first event in October 2016, has been powerful, courageous, change-making poetry.

At that first event, our attenders were privileged to hear the incredible work of Jo McFarlane and Sally Fox, whose poems are featured in this book. You could have heard a pin drop as their powerful messages touched the audience, many of whom later told us how profoundly they had been impacted, as well as inspired to 'do something' as a result.

Lucy and I realised at this point how important poetry was going to be at future AD4E events and so, as we travelled around the country, we invited more and more people to share their work. The performances of poetry and spoken word quickly became part of the fabric of the day and, in my view, are the heart of the whole event.

Many of the poets in this book have shared their poetry as part of the AD4E movement, live and/or at our online events. You can watch some of these performances (and others by poets we haven't managed to include here) on the A Disorder 4 Everyone YouTube channel, where we post clips from our various events (www.youtube.com/channel/UCaWG15Tqjo6sZ7obcn Kc_Mw) or via our website (adisorder4everyone.com).

As I said at the start, all of the contributors to this book want change. The words that you will read in these pages are an expression not only of this desire for change but also of a conscious decision to be part of that change. It is one of the many ways of 'doing something', of being a change-maker.

Jo Watson

References

Walker, A. (2013). *The cushion in the road: Meditation and wandering as the whole world awakens to being in harm's way.* New Press.

Watson, J. (2019). *Drop the disorder! Challenging the culture of psychiatric diagnosis.* PCCS Books.

Decolonising distress
Sanah Ahsan

this world will tell you
to keep your distress
in sealed letters of lips
behind shiny white envelopes
that no one need read.

they will stamp it
with a diagnosis.

label your suffering an illness.

they will call it
depression
while you call it
survival from oppression.

they will feed you pills
to cure social ills.

medicate injustice.

they will name the imbalance
of power in society
a chemical imbalance
of your brain.

refuse to understand the causes of your pain.

they will attempt to colonise the earth of your mind
with a language your mother tongue cannot swallow
and you will be lost in translation
searching for urdu subtitles
so your grandmother might understand.

they will offer terms like
Anxiety Disorder
and
Post Traumatic Stress Disorder

and
you will wonder
what this apparently ordered way of living is.

a filing of feelings into categories
of a cabinet
that cannot be contained.

but you must remember:
that this feeling is not a sickness.

remember:
they once called homosexuality an illness of the mind.

remember:
there was a time they labelled runaway slaves as being mentally ill
     for desiring freedom.

remember:
they still deem psychosis as a black and brown disease.

so please remember

and keep feeling.

cry on the tube in front of passing strangers. wear the cuts on
     your thighs like beautifully inked tattoos. put your sadness
     on like it is the silkiest shirt in your wardrobe. 2-step with
     the grief anchored to your feet like they're your freshest pair
     of Air Force Ones. let your tears fall in protest. release your
     rage in revolution to a world that is terrified of unedited
     and unfiltered truth.

do not dilute your heart. gather community around the table to
     feast in feeling.

let their sorrow and joy be a convoy
to ride each other out of this societal warfare.

show them your tenderness packs muscle, that this tenderness is
     shared

that this suffering is to be understood at the collective.
not only the individual perspective.

there is healing to be found at the level of community.

phenomenal woman, i am in love with your tenderness.

i am in love with our tenderness

stay tender

please, stay tender.

Fuck the DSM

Jyl Anais

Your medicine is
like a
weapon in disguise,

remote controlled
every morning religion.

It's no irony your pills look
like the bullets
they are:
dirty and dangerous.

I thought I needed them
like I thought I needed you
until I didn't anymore.

He said having them was like
having a gun in the house.
We couldn't wait to get you out.

I remember searching for a pill case
that could fit all of the medicine you'd
prescribed me, so I could
remember the regime
complicated routine

the chemical orchestra that helped line
your pockets
while you stole my time.

'Treatment' you called it
when it was you who poisoned me;
'Medicine', the thing that made me

continue to make appointment after appointment
all about those supposed illnesses you voted on
by committee.

Fuck you.
And fuck the DSM.

First published in Soft Out Spoken *(Sin Miedo Press, 2019)*

Burgundy
Jasmine Gardosi

I got my diagnosis.
I have burgundy.

It's a relief to know.
I'm not weak or lazy.
I have burgundy.

When people ask how I am today,
I tell them I have burgundy.
Sometimes I feel fine, but I know –
deep down – I have burgundy.

Burgundy goes with all of my clothes.

Nathan also has burgundy.
He takes Typtamine
for his burgundy.
I take Typtamine
for my burgundy, too.

Sarah says she has burgundy
but she drinks a lot and I don't.
I wonder at what stage of the burgundy
this will happen.

A friend of a friend had burgundy
but he took different tablets
to the ones my doctor gave me.
And then he stopped taking them.

And then he died,
and that makes me think,
will I die too, because I'm not
taking the tablets he took
to stop him being so burgundy?

Nathan's doctor was wrong.
He is not burgundy.

He actually has carmine.
They have started him
on Dozapram.

The Morrisons lady gave me
the wrong change and I cried,
probably because I have burgundy.

I saw a job I might really like,
but I don't think I'll apply,
because I have burgundy.

I have to stay in the bathroom
for a very long time when I see
my ex laughing with someone,
probably because I am burgundy.

I think burgundy
is my favourite colour.

First published in Hurtz *(Verve Poetry Press, 2019)*

I work within the crisis team
Amanda Bueno de Mesquita

I work within the crisis team,
Where clients don't have names.
Just diagnoses and their numbers,
Hence their heads are hung in shame.

Their details up on whiteboards,
Medications for review,
The homeless and the desperate,
Most seasoned and some new.

The workforce tap their notes up,
Feeding diagnostic lies the ink of truth,
And doctors look right through me
When I ask them for some proof.

I work within the crisis team,
Who visit clients bearing meds
To dampen out emotions
And gag the voices in their heads.

Wearing lanyards, giving leaflets,
And so few who truly care,
With ears that will not listen
To stories far from just or fair.

Yet trauma makes such sense to me,
When I stop by to sit and listen.
And suddenly some saddened eyes
Look into mine and glisten

Through their haze of medication,
That *harmecuticals* create.
I pray my conversations
Are not too little or too late.

As I gently tell those on my watch,
It makes sense to feel their pain.

As life has usually been cruel,
And there is no measure of sane.

I work within the crisis team,
And struggle to stay calm
When questioning the morality
Of iatrogenic harm.

I try to make a difference
In this world that's full of pain.
Where meds are understanding,
And where no one stands to gain.

Nocebo effect
Dr Julie Carter

He's been told he'll be on tablets
the rest of his life,
she's been told it's her age
'Wear and tear'.
Like an old Nissan Micra
her discs are worn out.
It just went for scrap
worth next to nowt.
She's been told to stop worrying
and give up the fags,
He's been told to lose weight
and stop drinking.
Knowing they should
but wondering how,
they're left all at sea
slowly sinking.

She's been told her depression is
chemistry all muddled up,
she should carry on
taking the tablets.
But he is psychotic
it's all in his genes,
it cannot be cured
only managed.
He's been told not to wait long
to write his will,
she's been told that
her chances are slim.
The disease is aggressive
it's probably spread
won't be long now
until they're both dead.
Who are the tellers
of tellings so bold

the knowers of knowledge and science?
Who are the wise ones
kind killers of hope,
respectable wearers
of medicine's white cloak?

He's been told he'll be on tablets
the rest of his life,
she's been told it's her age
'Wear and tear'.
The script has been written
the story is clear
awake late at night
slowly dying of fear.

Still they carry a lingering feeling
that somewhere
inside them
there's healing.

First published in Is it Serious? *(Mindfell, 2018)*

Tilt
Ruth E. Dixon

Wait no longer cherished child,
You are home where you belong,
A finding place where lonely doves gather,
Before carrying on.

Where surely we repair the shipwreck of our dreams,
When shame soaked through my lifeblood into you,
Like shattered bones on tracks of steel were ripped apart,
How? We couldn't say, we never knew.

My chaos and the constant mutilation,
Empty and carved out like carbons tossed
Across the concrete from where you could but turn on heel,
For those who run the fastest are most lost.

Abandoned by the forces that should have made you strong,
Confused by those who said there was something organically wrong
With me, a chemical imbalance, when all along it was to be,
This haunting counter-narrative slowly poisoning me.

The agony of stories borne and festering untold,
We cannot help how long it takes for trauma to unfold,
For darling, though it's rude to swear, I need to for this line:
The brainfuckers fuck us up and unfucking it all takes time.

Then in turn abuses met by those who still won't see,
Oppression at the heart of labels medically
Assigned by powers whose purpose to be proven wise,
Masks the bitter twist that they know less than they will ever
    realise.

The dreads of which they smother under their wolf skin vesture,
Those munching bulls wary of any sudden gesture,
 of kinship from strangers, when our only endeavour,
Is to honour that all of us are in this together.

Hold grief in your left hand and gratitude in right,

There is no room to carry guilt or blame,
We choose our joys and sorrows long before we live them,
And to turn back time, I'd choose them just the same.
Remember when we bought a TV dinner?
A Chinese takeaway of rice and sweet and sour pork,
And there we sat with metal tins at my little wooden table,
Enchanted by the skills on centre court,
At Wimbledon that summer that was to be my last,
The sadness smashed so hard right through the core,
But it marked our capacity for joy so ours was endless,
And side by side I couldn't have asked for more.
To live a life not broken by the system,
To live a life not beaten by those who too easily scare,
But just to be together with my daughter,
That was my life, that was my life right there.

The rest which can't be spoken will emerge,
Resist the urge to spell it out in black and white,
But use it in the way you feel a person's struggle,
And how you listen to every beat in spite,
The fact the story's in the silence, in the margins of the frame,
For that which is unspoken will rise again.

So in a moment turn around, the end is yours and yours alone,
And trust that, though you need to turn, I am still with you,
And in that way you're never on our own,
To bring my left hand with your right,
Together as you learn to find the notes and play,
Tethered to your kite strings, to fly but not to fade away.

Remember me as though we are still dancing,
Immersed in our electrifying swirl,
Beholden as we are to no one but each other,
Sparkling with the spirit of what it is to be a girl.

Remember me when dancing with your daughter,
In open heart she hears your every truth,
Then takes you by the hand to share new rhythms,
How bright the future shines, my dearest Ruth.
Wait no longer, cherished child,

Here's where I bid you goodbye,
Let wounded souls weep,
Every woman must die.
But to capture the essence,
Of all that is and once was,
To bend into being,
To bend into because,
Life is to be taken at the tilt,
What use are we if merely to be still?
When beyond the wilds at the reaches of the unknown,
Is where we learn to tilt, to tilt until,
We lean a little further into all we might become,
The edge where I still hover to will to be your mum,
I am a mum who's reaching with you,
To catch you when you fall,
For a life that's taken at the tilt,
Is the place where we stand tall,
We are the giants who always remain humble,
We are the warriors who dare to leave the shore,
We are survivors whose stories we shall honour,
We are the people we've been waiting for.

More and less all of this
Lydia Daisy

I am an ocean
I happen in waves
Motions and emotions
I feel things so deeply

I am easily moved
I usually mean even more than I say
I often say a hell and heaven of a lot
Agenda-ed or without plot
Then at points, peaks, troughs and others
I'd rather not.

I long to be,
or no...
– well, you know
But do you?
I do
I don't
I'm up there
I'm down there
and do apathy so well

Sometimes I feel everything
Sometimes I feel nothing
Sometimes I'm sure I am everything
Sometimes I'm sure I am nothing
Sometimes I want everything
Sometimes I want nothing
And this is infinite
It is not egotistical to say that I am also

The very same action or reaction
Can sit and live in a million different bits in me
Frequently, all at three times
It can be slow and backward in other lines

Finite is Euphoria
But no one ever cried forever either

Living in my land,
It's enough to whelm you to implosion and the opposite
    effortlessly
Had enough to understand
That conflicting truths are extremely able to exist and happen
    concurrently
I am more equipped
Because I've seen and been
In more edges and stripes
In this very short life
Than you ever knew there were

We only have our experiences and mine are freaking huge
Muting something won't stop it from happening
Silencing is not enough to remove
Sure, it can be dangerous to be me
But painkillers don't stop the bleeding you see

So I try to remain linear
Don't fix her
Just see her
I aim for acceptance
To find the time to understand them individually
No pretence
Just this tense
The gift

I live through this heart
And so adore art
So mobile
I dive into smiles and bile
Inside me so much
I will paint to touch
You
I express
Not only because it leaks from me

But also because it all connects
My chest's best in sets
Even opposites reflect

I'm mostly deep
Some drown in my speech
Such fun at edges, then I'll pull you gravitationally to seek
It doesn't take a genius.
Understanding can also lift and assist on both sides

And here's something I have learnt
From being lit and getting burnt,
You can have this for free – damn it's mine
But most of the time
I'm aware
All I want is to do share,
The waves...
They will never, ever, ever, stop coming

I believe meaning is in moving
Changing and exchanging
Because it will happen anyway

So don't you ever, ever, ever dare vignette my peripheral
Who knows how long I'll have these eyes and they are beautiful
Just like all of it

I am so seeing and being, enantiodromia inevitable

And you know
That you must let me go
Let me flow
So like the waves that I am
Sure, remind me of the ground
And please know that I am around
But you cannot tell me what I am
Because you would be wrong.

Because I am more and less, all of this.

I am an ocean
I happen in waves
Motions and emotions
I feel so deeply

I am all of this.
And more
And less
And more
And less
And more
And less
And more
And less
And more
And less

Self-discovery
Mica Gray

when I tell you
that aliens have implanted
chips in my head
or that the CIA is leaving microphones
under my bed
that I
think I am Jesus.
don't get caught up on the metaphors.

don't try to take my poetry
and fit it into your theory of psychology
in attempt
to calculate how far away i am
from the normal way that a human being
ought to relate to itself
don't lock me into your narrow definitions of good mental
     health.
no, I don't actually think that I am Jesus of Nazareth
who walked the desert for 40 days
and brought salvation through death.
what I am trying to communicate
is that I now recognise myself,
as important.
as having a cross to bear.
as a being made of love.
as a being, with a great purpose.
as a being, with a strong spirit.
so don't get upset
when i refuse to let you convince me
that it is irrational to feel like a God
when i have finally encountered
a sense of divinity
within me.
when i have promised myself
to no longer let

the demons, the CIA, the aliens,
my negative thoughts
win in their attempt to
put out my fire.

so, when I tell you
that I am fighting the aliens in my head,
that I'm getting rid of the microphones
that the CIA have put under my bed
that I
feel like Jesus.
don't get caught on the metaphors.
simply reply,
it's about time.

First published in The Colour of Madness *(Stirling Publishing, 2018)*
and When Daisies Talk *(Kindle Direct Publishing, 2019)*

Drop the disorder!
Jo Watson

Drop the disorder
drop it hard
with intent
let it fall
crashing down
on a hard vengeful floor
witness it
fragmenting into shameful pieces
that we can stamp on
dance on
then sweep into the pile of other toxic dirt
that we collected earlier.

Drop the dehumanising
the othering
and smothering
with victim blaming tactics
stealing stories
and swapping them for lies
and an arrogance that puts money on us not noticing
but we do

Drop the deceit
the manipulation of data
fuelling pseudo-scientific bullshit
like nothing else could
buying answers and truths
at committees' requests

Drop the invaliding
insidious inferences of irrelevance
that disconnect, separate
because you know that
unlinked stories
evaporate
conveniently

to a state of no-threat
Drop the scapegoating
individualising
tick-box trickery
with diseases to confirm
it's no one's fault
so that discriminations,
inequalities
atrocities
and neglect
are all nicely protected

Drop the disorder
drop it hard
with intent
let it fall
crashing down
on a hard vengeful floor
witness it
fragmenting into shameful pieces
that we can stamp on
dance on
then sweep into the pile of other toxic dirt
that we collected earlier.

Act of war
Jyl Anais

Your men raped
a woman
in uniform
and then, again
and again,
one who offered
you intelligence
and service
so that she could afford
an education.

Then, you diagnosed her
with a 'personality disorder'.

No/wait, don't tell me
she had an underlying/
illness
that hadn't been diagnosed,
one that went undetected before.

She enlisted   ready
to serve her country
and boy did she ever,
on her knees,
before you silenced her
with a code
that cannot be spoken
aloud
or printed for fear
of reprisal.

Was it 301.83?
Was she angry
humiliated
made powerless
by overwhelming
force?

Couldn't she
contain herself
anymore?
Did she become hysterical?

Was she terrified of you?
And did you note
her 'paranoia'
in shorthand
on your yellow legal pad?
Were you scared of her?
Did she feel empty
after you took everything
away?
Did she want to leave
the Earth
this life
after she realised
who you really were
and what you were capable of?
Did she forget who she was?
Could she still recognize her own
reflection once you were finished
using her?
Did you find her behavior
toward you
inappropriate?

Rape is an act of   war,
a form of   torture.
Was she your   prisoner?

Or was it 313.81?
Was she rude?
Didn't she follow your orders?
Did she resent your men?
Or did you consider that she said 'No'
at all
an act of insubordination?

Your judgments
translate into indelible codes
that prevent
her future employment.

Or was she 'Honorably Discharged'
to/ protect your own?

Tell me again
that psychiatry isn't a form of
social control,
that you didn't intend for those codes
to act as the kind of insurance
that ensures silence
you cannot buy
any
other
way.

First published in Soft Out Spoken *(Sin Miedo Press, 2019)*

On the inside
Martha Enticott

When Martha performed this piece at a Drop the Disorder online poetry evening, she said:
'I'd like to dedicate my poem tonight to all the children who are locked away within a psychiatric unit or who have been traumatised by the time that they have spent inside. I also dedicate my poem to all the children who have had their voices taken away and are sadly no longer with us today. In particular, one special girl who has left a light on in the world and in everyone's hearts. I will carry her around and fight for change. Rest peacefully, Manon.'

I'm going to tell about a place no child should go.
Somewhere that drains your soul hollow
And sadness follows you round like it's your shadow

In this place every door that opens will lock behind you.
And you're treated like a caged wild animal in a zoo,
Locked up with no hope of rescue.

Everything that is potentially harmful is stuck to the ground,
No pencils or crayons are anywhere to be found,
All hope of normality is drowned.

So out of control that you're detained by the law,
And you're made to take meds that make you withdraw,
You're forcibly held and treated like an outlaw.

As soon as you arrive all your belongings are snatched away,
The most meaningful possessions are hidden from you until your
     release day,
Yet they expect you to act like you're okay.

You're stripped of your power and voice,
And the treatment you get is not your choice,
It seems like until you die they won't get your point.

You're allowed to see family for one hour on visiting days,
But if you misbehave they'll take that time away,
So for the love of God just do what they say.

When you get angry they'll drag you to the seclusion room,
'They're nothing but a troublesome, violent teenager' they
    assume,
But in reality your mind is poisoned with doom and gloom.

If you don't eat your dinner then they won't let you see your
    family,
It's funny how you're shown no love when you're hurting
    physically and mentally,
If you don't agree with a doctor they'll call you a spoilt brat
    continually.

When it's time to go to sleep there's no one to say goodnight,
You become afraid to fall asleep because your mind is full of
    fright,
And when you're scared and alone no one is there to tuck you in
    tight.

You can scream for help at the top of your lungs,
But even then they won't listen to your feelings,
Because as far as they're concerned you're not a human being.

It may shock you to hear that I'm not talking about a prison,
Instead it's the place where the sad, mad and bad are hidden,
I'm talking about a psychiatric unit, a place with no compassion.

Open the can of worms

Tracey Farrell

This poem was written by Tracey after speaking to many survivors about their experiences of mental health services and practitioners who described asking about trauma histories as 'opening a can of worms'.

I heard you talking as I was walking
by your open door
Telling each other to
stick to the presenting issue,
Don't go opening a can of worms
keep to our core
Let's do this on our terms
Yet you don't realise that this can of worms
That you don't want to open
Stays stuck inside of me
wriggling and squirming,
gnawing and chewing
Eating away at my insides
with each toxic bite,
until I learn to fight and show my might
through snide words and worse
Or worse still, till I have no fight left,
no will to live,
no reason at all
And I wonder
Do you remember my name?
That I told you my dad
died by suicide when I was five?
Do you smile when you see me, or roll your eyes?
That dread you feel as you
answer your phone
and the receptionist says in that tone,
the one reserved by people

like her for people like me
'It's her… again'
'Give me ten,' you sigh
and then wonder why
I scream at her and hang up,
not just the phone but this time
my never-to-return sign.
So my appointment arrives and I don't arrive,
and you note with rising glee
a DNA or an FTA on that file of my life
I wonder what might happen
if instead of that being attributed to me,
it was attributed to you.
What would you do?
If that failure to attend meant
You failed to attend
to trauma-informed practices
that might have made the difference
and if I didn't have to pretend
to care about your therapy
With their cute little acronyms
ACT, CBT, and DBT
All the letters except M and E
Me
I want you to see me… work well with me,
and open that can of worms
Not to watch you squirm but to help me see
That I am not rotten,
That my 'mental illness' and my addictions
Are just a symptoms of trauma not forgotten
My body, it remembers
Even when my mind can't join the dots
From a to b and to c
See?
It's your way, or the highway
With your policies full of risk adversity
That trump the ones about trauma
And make me jump

Through hoops made of government red tape
Believe me
I know it's not just you, it's the whole system
I don't expect
Blue tights and a cape
You don't have to save me
But it would help if you'd see me
Through a lens of understanding
And take time to develop
Relationship
Built on trust
so that when you do what you must
The scales might tip
Towards me being supported and vindicated
And you could ask and respond,
rather than tell and react
So that I can learn to ask
for what I need and respond
with my truth rather than tell you
what I think you want to hear
and to stop me reacting from my trauma,
so far out of my Window of Tolerance
Zero tolerance
Isn't just a poster on a wall
Warning me that you require safety
It's how you and I feel about
My sadness and pain
no tolerance at all
So it masquerades as rage
And fills the page you write about me
Confirming my non-compliance
With the treatment that you do to me
I'm trapped in your paragraph prison
There's precision in the way you wield that pen
Severing the human parts of me
Without me ever having made a decision
About how it would be
How I wish I could be openly defiant

To ask for what I need
Just open the can of worms
Barriers exist that you can't even see
They stand rock solid before me
Telling me that no one cares
So when you run late it just confirms
the worm of self-hate
Crawling through my mind
That it is all on your terms
And those terms are clear
You can see my fate
Mood states turned to personality traits
The doctor has ordered
My mind disordered
Borderline, Antisocial...
ain't so far from the truth
If we're talking about the mess
That is my social engagement system
shot to pieces by toxic stress
Where rules about my body got broken
By people who said rules shouldn't get broken
At least not by me
And here I am breaking rules again
Speaking the unspoken,
Asking you to see
That the one tool you need
Is this –
Open the can of worms!

*First published on www.madintheuk.com (11 January, 2019)
and https://medium.com/@ascaaustralia (21 March, 2019)*

The Killing of Susan Kelly
Dorothy Dundas

The dark-suited man slithered,
Shock box in hand,
To our bedsides, four girls, innocent, naked,
Waiting... waiting... waiting,
Sticky-headed,
One by one.
Zapping currents through us,
Young bones cracked, brains bruised
By his cold-fingered electrified touch.
Crime completed,
In collusion with white-skirted nurses,
The limb holders,
He slinked back into the early morning frost,
Steaming hot coffee in hand,
Leaving us quieted, flat as pancakes.
And Susan,
The soft white sheet covering her,
Did not move at all.
His shocks had stolen her, skin and bone,
That beautiful flaxen-haired child,
At seventeen,
Silencing her questioning stream
Of daily chatter, her ballet dreams.
In her innocence, she had spoken for me,
muted and crushed by endless sizzlings.
Inches away, I did not hear her silent call
As she slipped into death's embrace,
Beyond –
Where her little fingers hold the violin
strings to my heart,
Playing them like a marionette
In the gentle breezes of heaven.

First published on www.madinamerica.com (2019)

Crazier than me
(A poem for all those who still administer ECT)
Ruth E. Dixon

Crazy is what you pin on me,
But crazy is giving ECT,
Crazy, the world's gone crazy,
And you are way more crazier than me!

It's quite judgemental,
To call you mental,
And I should rise above the labels that you pin on me,
We, could leave things be,
If it weren't so completely crazy.

E,
C,
T,
CRAZY,
Way more crazier than me!

Crazy is what you pin on me,
But crazy is giving ECT,
Crazy, the world's gone crazy,

And you are way more crazier than me!
You are way more crazier than me!

Everyday magic
Dr Julie Carter

How do you heal a heart that is broken?
You stitch it up
With love in time
How do you say what cannot be spoken?
You weave it
In a verse and rhyme

So if I could tell you
The reason why I wake
And take just one more breath
If I could tell you
Of the life inside me
The blood that's pulsed
Inside my chest

Then I'd tell you a story
Of everyday magic
Of sunset and moonrise
And sea-washed sand
Of how I live on the courage I borrow
Every time you reach out your hand

From the everyday magic
Of teacups and teardrops
From wagging tails and runs in the rain
Is spun the thread to stitch my heart up
So I live and love
And breathe again

First published in Is it Serious? *(Mindfell, 2018)*

I mistook myself for a scientific label
Dr Peter Gordon

This is neither fact
nor expert advice:
I am an artist, a poet, and all that may be in between.
This is neither fact
nor expert advice:
Specialisms are making nonsense of sense.
We are being divided.

First published on www.madinamerica.com (17 April, 2018)

Dis-ease

Kathleen Halley Angus

Dis-ease
A sickness in the mind
They look at me with pity
'Don't worry, with this medicine, you'll get better in time'

Dis-ease
A sickness in the mind
I see they're numb.
With a desire to help but a refusal to look inside
Too afraid to question the foundations of their thought
In fear of what they'll find
So they turned people into patients
And built a world upon a lie

Dis-ease
A sickness in the mind
'You're not well,
You slashed your wrists and tried to die,
You say you want to disappear'
    Yes, but only 'cus I saw the truth
    And it hurt so much I couldn't bear to stay here

Dis-ease
A sickness in the mind
'You're delusional' they say
'You're obsessed with your face'
    No, I'm letting go
    I'm waking up
    I'm going home
And you're still lost in space

Don't you think it's funny we're so ill at ease?
Don't you think it's strange?
Could it be because we're just not yet at peace?
Could it be that it's our perspective that needs to change?

Dis-ease
A sickness in the mind
'Shush, take the drugs, they'll help you.'
   Not true
   Numb you is what they'll do.

They don't want the truth though, see
Because if madness is healing
What does that make sanity?

No apology in pathology
Sally Fox

They never say sorry when they get it wrong
even though you told them all along.

You didn't quite agree
But technically that isn't disagreeing
Still compliant
Just questioning
not defiant.

Twelve psychiatrists later
and a decade lost to medication and side effects…
Finally I am listened to,
having evidenced with detailed mood charts
It feels like respect
But instead, a new diagnosis is given

It's not so much mood as behaviour driven.
Personality Disorder! And Borderline at that!
'What about Bipolar? Do they overlap?'

They can co-exist
But there's the matter of your manias…
They're not quite long enough, she said

So I'm a borderline Bipolar
'Can I come off my meds?'

A solemn expression followed by:
I wouldn't recommend it

'Well I really want to. Can't we at least try it?'

Epilim was the first to go
and signs of mania started to show:
Elation caused by the drug's withdrawal.
We slowed down the process
to a gentler regime.
Next to go was Lamotrigine –
a cautious and careful wean.

Two years later I'm mood-stabiliser free
and I've completed three years in DBT

In remission and recovery
Everyone's so proud of me
But, that damn label is still stuck to me.
There really is no apology in pathology.

First published in Stigma and Stones: poems on living
with a diagnosis of BPD *(2014)*

Six verses
Viv Gordon

I get six sessions
To answer a lifetime
Spent floating outside myself trying to come in

I have six reasons
To stay in this body
But I cannot remember them not even one

It takes six minutes
To tick all her boxes
How food is a nonsense and still I can't sleep

I have six hours with
The woman, her training
Her offerings of labels and drugs I don't want

It takes six seconds
To absorb her word 'stuck'
And to watch myself drowning engulfed in its wake

I have six words to
Spit back at the woman
Evidence and outcomes and fuck you you arsehole

I have six months which
I don't think I'll last through
I'm staring at nothing and brick walls and nooses

I have six women
Who hold my heart gently
Who tell me I matter until I believe them

I have six songs now
I sing to the women
They all start with hope and they all end with change

A penny dropped
Ruth E. Dixon

To lose the mum that never was,
To miss what is unknown because,
The mum that never was, was not,
An empty chair that time forgot.

To ask in death this passing shot:
Who is my mum, why was she not?
How can she sit upon a chair,
And yet the world knows not she's there?

She must be so, she might be missed,
But so she must for I exist,
Where is it that no light is shone?
Who is my mum, why has she gone?

Beware the truths we seek to find,
The melting icebergs of our mind,
For once a tipping penny drops,
A penny dropped undropped cannot.

And penny dropped serves pounds to fall,
Cascading waves crush weathered wall,
A tide of knowns so come to bear,
A mother lost but she is there.

She floats between the drifting leaves,
And sweeps across the summer breeze,
Flying freely to the hills,
Then shines amongst the daffodils.

She calls to me in beats unbroken,
This earth at last where fears are spoken,
And whispers what I always knew,
'Hashtag my dear, hashtag me too.'

And so the mum that never was,
Becomes herself, becomes because,
Her constellation can but glisten,
We hear her for we chose to listen.

To all her hurt and shattered dreams,
To all the vaults she filled with screams,
To all her vibrancy unseen,
To all we lost that might have been.

I should have known but I did not,
We must have heard but we forgot,
To listen to the silent child,
We thought her mad, we called her wild.

They gave her tablets, shocks and scares,
They told her off, they went downstairs,
And left her in an empty chair,
So she was lost but she was there.

She fought against the mounting tide,
She fought to live, she really tried,
To find a way to come inside,
But they kept her out and so she died.

Forgive me mum I did not know,
Forgive me mum I did not go,
It's just I knew not what to do,
Your agony, I felt it too.

I felt it too, hashtag me too,
It wasn't half as bad as you,
And yet the parts make up the sum,
It kills me for you are my mum.

So tell me planet, tell me sea,
When do we rise, when can we be
The stories our unique lives tell?
A person heard can heal, be well.

This turning crest her parting gift,
The hope from wounds one day we lift,
'For change,' she echoes, 'can't be stopped,
A penny dropped undropped cannot.'

When daisies talk
Mica Gray

violets are red
roses are blue
and last night
i had a dream while awake
that i was walking with Adam and Eve
past birds and butterflies
purple skies and blue trees.
and in a moment of self-perception
in a river's reflection
i saw that eve was she
and she was me
and we were being led to a door
inside of a fruit tree.

i entered in
tentatively
and as i pressed my feet against the earth
i heard a voice whisper a word
a daisy,
telling me to lend my ear to her.
despite my fear that daisies could talk
in that moment
i knew I could not ignore her call.
so i bent real low, and she spoke real slow
and told me all the things of life
she thought I should know.
she told me that blood runs throughout all the earths veins
and that there are secret melodies hidden inside the worlds rain
she told me that there is a God that hears every moan and groan
that she herself had heard the call of my soul
echoed in the emptiness within me that has been yearning
to be whole.
she told me that underneath the shadow of life
there is a network,
comprised of all the things that share the will to be.
the birds, the stars, the planets, the trees

are all connected in a web of deep intricacy
and all that seems separate is really part of the one
and now that i have entered this knowing
my real education has begun.
she said that only in losing my will to live
have i been able to find it.
only in losing myself, have i been able to find me.
she told me, that I exist
to bring the love from heaven
onto this earth
and that i had gone wrong in this life
by letting this world question my self-worth
feeding myself to death with knowledge
spending too much time trying to prove to other people
who are trying to prove to other people
that they are worth something
without ever really just being.

and when she finished speaking
she swept the tears from my eyes
wrapped her vines around my arms
held me tight between her leaves
and in that stillness
taught me how to breathe

inhale
exhale.

she taught me how to be
simply me
naturally.

and when I woke from that blessed reality
i overheard from my hospital bed
it was delusion
psychosis, they said.
a manifestation of the degradation of this young girl's mind
or, something similar along those lines
but nothing about me now seeing through spiritual eyes
and seeing through all of the world's most precious lies.

bad is not good. good is not bad. mad is not sane. insane is not mad.
war is not peace. sin is not freedom. happiness is not fear.
apathy is not love.
i wonder how many other voices
making their way through this confusion
have been crushed by narratives of delusion
as carelessly as daises are trampled in the field
destroyed before they could blossom
uprooted before they could heal
i wish that people would listen when daisies talk
and value the stories of those in psychiatric wards
and hear the secrets of soul that are whispered between those walls.
bad is not good. good is not bad. mad is not sane. insane is not mad.
I wish that people would listen when daisies talk
and not persist in locking us into fictional ideas of sanity
closing their ears
out of the fear
of confronting their own vulnerability.

i am ever grateful for those
who have come before me to study humanity
from within and outside the boundaries of psychiatry
and shown the place beneath the psyche
where the seeds of ego are sewn
who found that in that place the ground does not devour you whole
but folds you in its embrace
in order for a rebirthing to take place.

i'm grateful to those
who listened to daisies speak
because they taught me
i don't have to hate myself
or label my experience in the tree as disease
but that i can see it as a natural part of my development
necessary for my growing
spiritually.

First published in When Daisies Talk *(Kindle Direct Publishing, 2019)*

Jump start
Jyl Anais

The professionals act like
the theft   of half my life was
    no
        big
            deal
because they didn't mean to.
In a cloak of benevolence
under the guise of medicine

/ help / undercover
and POOF!
twenty years
      gone
           just
                like
that.
My anger
no longer a symptom once
I left the reservation.

So, now what?
I challenge their ideas
and practices,
me with my brain still just intact enough
to recollect.
Me, with anger enlivening my eyes
while I sit in their waiting rooms
like a threat.

They try and calm me
with kindness
they bill for and
take notes about
except I'm not in confession
anymore.

I know this is
                    not
            my
church.
I've got to jump start my life
again like I've had to
before,
and begin
            again,
                        and again,
        and again.

First published on www.madinamerica.com (28 June, 2018) and then in Soft Out Spoken *(Sin Miedo Press, 2019)*

I remember
Wend Badger

I remember…
us
always us... never walking, always racing to
the next adventure; the next mountain to climb, baddie to kill
every space filled with a pirate ship, a cowboy ranch, a rocket
never a moment… always an escapade

I remember…
when
you stopped racing to and began running from
a fear that you owned no words to describe
and the pirates, spaceships, cowboys were children's games now…
we shared them, still... because we were children, still
but they were different. Because inside you were leaving us

I remember…
that
subtle change to your eyes, the hardening of your jaw the
slow construction of the iron bars around your soul
and your loving, happy innocence being engulfed, drowned
your beautiful spark becoming hotter... becoming rage

I remember…
how
the pain became blood;
an unheard scream
met instead with impassionate diagnoses
hard words out of a revered and baseless book
that existed only to pathologise pain

I remember…
your
name; married now to a disorder, a scaling back of you
of your story
that could not be heard against the din
of psychiatric pronouncement
and judgement

I remember...
those
impersonal, technical words
became hard white pills
so many, many pills that took you further away
but never removed that which pursued you

I remember...
when
those thousand doses became one
to be taken late at night, alone
when the medical terms given proved no defence
against the pain screaming and raging inside you

And you found a way to make it quiet

I remember.
You.

They think

A. Hurford

They think they know you know
They think they do
They've got what they've heard
Such reliable word
That they think they know
All about you

So they'll act and imply
Without fear of reply
As no one ever bothered
To put it to you

They are quite certain
They know who you are
Though the who gets lost
You're now more of a what
As they comment around and about
Thoughtless of you

They seem to rely
On a fear to reply
That you're dumb to their jibes
That real life passes you by

They think you're wrong about you
That you're not true
That you'd be you
If you were their you
If only you knew how to be you

But they don't know

You do

All of this disorder stuff
Jo Watson

All of this 'disorder' stuff
Just in case you're not aware
Is absolutely, unequivocally
Bloody everywhere

And if you think I'm joking
Or not quite on the money
You'd be wrong and I'd be right
And it ain't even funny

Cos I'm telling you it's in the books
The papers and the journals
It's in the main gists and the subtexts
It's both inside and external

The words are automatic
They are default they are 'go-to'
We've absorbed them all as normal
Chatting them as though they're true

Plethoras of diagnoses
With acronyms to boot
Accepted as real illnesses
With nothing to dispute

For most it's not a thought
That it's a made-up crock of shite
Psychiatry's approved it all
So the science must be right!

But the moment you dig deeper
It starts falling into place
The lies and motivations
Just stare you in the face

Look into my eyes
Sue Irwin

'My poem is in the form of a letter to the mental health system that I reached out to for help; a system that viewed my responses to abuse as symptoms of an illness; a system that then sucked me in, labelled me, medicated me and shocked me; a system that did me more harm than good, then spat me out, leaving me to pick up the pieces.'

When you're done with noting down the colour of my skin, the
      style of my hair, my gender, the clothes I'm wearing, the
      way I sit,
When you're done with judging the way I express myself, the way
      I behave,
When you're done with calculating the risk I pose to you,
When you're done with depriving me of my freedom,
When you're done with stripping away my dignity, my
      humanity, my self-agency,
When you're done with labelling me and placing me in one of
      your cluster groups,
When you're done with plotting out your pathway for me,
When you're done with subtly insisting on my compliance to
      your world,
When you're done with inflicting upon me your evidence-based
      practices and lecturing me about your NICE guidelines,
When you're done with questioning the very core of me,
When you're done with blaming me and shaming me,
When you're done with crushing my hopes and my dreams,
When you're done with raping my soul and breaking my spirit,
When you're done with killing me softly,
When you're done with all this,
I would ask you,
To show me your humility, your willingness to learn,
To put down your textbooks, your manuals and your formularies,
To set aside your prescription pads,

To peel off the electrodes you've placed on my forehead,
To remove your clouded spectacles,
And to step down from your thrones of power,
And when you are ready,
I invite you to be with me in my world,
To walk alongside me as I stumble along my fragile pathway,
To share with me your vulnerability as I have shared with you mine,
To sit with me and bear witness to my hopelessness, my alienation,
    my pain, my sense of betrayal, my grief and my humiliation,
To look into my eyes,
Where you will see the child within me who holds the agony, the
    scars, the terror, the silent screams,
And when you have sat for a while with all that you have witnessed,
And are able and willing to hold this space and explore with me
    my story,
Then my self-loathing, my despair, my loneliness, my shame, my
    fear begins to fade and wither,
My spirit begins to awaken, and my soul begins to heal.
Only then might you begin to understand who I am.

Smart move
Jackie Hagan

You know how people hear voices?
Well i hear applause,
it must be when i need it
it's mental health gone right.

The body and mind are always trying to heal itself,
and sometime when the traditionally healthy way isn't available
it does it in weird way.

There's a mental health diagnosis called 'Borderline Personality
        Disorder',
they give it to women and girls when they don't know why we're
        acting
different to them,
one of the traits of BPD is being manipulative,
this is seen by doctors as right out bad.

But, if the person
or system
that has what you need
(be that love or validation or a roof over your head or food)
isn't playing fair
then being manipulative is the smart move you are forced into.

To get by
sometimes people cheat, steal, are passive aggressive, lie,
sometimes someone is bombarded with endless messages and
        advertising
that you should have status
and you are pissed off with the unfair hand you're dealt
and you walk down market street
and all the windows have been smashed through,
so you pick up a pair of trainers.

In the Manchester lootings in 2011
it was the trainer shops, the mobile phone shops that got
        looted,

trainers and phones are things that give you status when you've
   got none

The poshest shop, Selfridges
did not get looted.
it got set on fire.

It could have been me
Jen Yates

It could have been me.
I'm the lucky one
To have escaped the clutches of 'Services'.

It nearly was me.
At 21, a close call
After attempting to end it all.

My friends saved me,
From the psychiatrist's questions and said defiantly…
'We'll take care of her.'

Therapists helped me.
We gave a narrative to my early bereavements, trauma and sexual
   violence.
Explorations that liberated and healed me.

I was fortunate.

My brother wasn't so lucky.
His decades of shrinks and meds.
Different diagnoses. Pain. Distress.

Judgment, police, no support. Locked up.
No care, just papering the symptoms chemically.
I feel so sad and angry it was him.

Their psychotropic cosh
Has taken him away somewhat.
My lovely bro – still here yet sometimes so far away.

And yet, there is hope with 'Drop the Disorder'
A group of like-minded warriors.
Pushing away this diagnostic culture that damages so.

I feel the ground swelling
With passionate and energised voices.
Singing their truth to the powers that shouldn't be.

Not being silenced for a moment longer.
Creatively banging the drum for compassion and change.
To ask about lives, not symptoms.

It could have been me.
And in a small way it was...
I live his trauma and pain vicariously.

I'd love to see him free
From the chemical lobotomy...
So he can say 'It was – but it's no longer me.'

Drop the disorder haiku
Amanda Bueno de Mesquita

Communication
When the words get in the way
Elephants cry too

* * *

A diagnosis
Of the narrative of life
Sticks pins in my soul

* * *

Anaesthetising
Trauma with medication
You are the dis-ease

* * *

Pharmaceutical
Biochemical weapon
Drop the Disorder

I can see you (but you are so very far away)
Ruth Jackson

I can see you
But you are so very far away
Obscured by screens, curtains and others
By drugs that blur your edges
And stories that redefine, define and divide you (and me)

I can hear you
But you are so very far away
Words are faint, broken and fractured
By definitions, diagnosis and disorders
By stories that silence, distance and disrupt you (and me)

I can feel you
But you are so very far away
Driven across corridors, wards and treatment rooms
By detachment, disassociation, and depersonalisation
Stories that neutered and vivisected you (and me)

I can taste you
But you are so very far away
Salt stale sweat, cheap disinfectant, rancid fear leaking from you
Nothing there is sweet, or fresh, no lime juice or basil
Stories have been purged of your richness (and mine)

There is no healing here, for you (or me)
No recognition of who you are, of your life, of what happened to
        you (or me)
Of all that you are, in your beautiful complexity
They are looking in all the wrong places
In all the wrong ways

So, let us bring you home
Let us reclaim you to this world

And we will wash you and love you
Feed you and listen
Tend to the pain rooted in your life,

not manifested in your brain (or mine)
And together, in time, we will find our way
to live our life, know and tell our own stories
And finally, woven together, we will begin to mend

Let's stop pretending
Brian E. Levitt

DSM 1 isn't real.
Have you read it?
Have you allowed yourself time travel
to Mind Fuck Number 1?
Ground Zero?
I've read it.
I'm a time traveler.
Let me tell you what I've seen.
It's very simple:
it isn't real.
It was replaced by 2 and 3 and 3R
and 4 and 4TR and 5.
And I've read them all.
And not one of them is real.
No matter how high the number grows
they are not real.

And I've been asked to swear an oath
on these shifting sands.
Labels that don't stand still.
Labels that flatten everything in their path.
Labels that flatten life
until it is unrecognizable.
Labels that are poison,
quick and slow.
Labels that don't make sense.
Labels that blind and confuse and confound.
Labels that don't define me.
Labels that don't define you.
Labels that can't possibly ever define anyone.
Labels that can't be
any
one
Person.
Labels will never breathe

and be
a precious life trying to make sense
and simply live.

Labels are not real.

I've been taught them
tested on them
trained in them
and accosted by them
day after day.
I know what they mean.
I can speak the language.
I'm fluent in Mind Fuck.
I know how they're used
and I refuse
to swear the oath.
They are not real.

Distress is real.

Your distress is real.
My distress is real.
It can never be contained
constrained
or explained
by a label.
It is alive in you.
It is alive in me.
It can never be named by a book
or a panel of doctors
or a single doctor
or anyone else.

No one can name you
or me.
Their names for us are not real.

The names we find
and choose

for ourselves,
the names we choose
to inhabit,
those are real.
I want to know your chosen names,
and if you find new names
I want to know those, too.

Your favourite theory isn't real.
CBT
Psychodynamic
Existential
Not real.
The Tribes
of the Person-Centred Approach,
they are not fucking real.
It's time to grow up now
and see
they are not real.
The Tribes
are a mind fuck,
a racist appropriation
of a word that's not ours.
It Balkanizes a duality
(Directive and Non-Directive),
and fuels fights
we call debates –
pissing contests.
And Directivity is not real.
And Non-Directivity is not real.
And we've all been fooled
if we think they are real.
Theoretical approaches are all lies.
They are not real.

Don't sacrifice your life
your one precious life
your individuality

your personal power
on the altar
of something that isn't real.

Freud isn't real.
Jung isn't real.
Skinner,
not real.
Don't get me wrong,
they lived
they breathed
they wrote
they were real.
And then we made them
each of them
into something unreal
while they were still alive
and breathing
and writing
and speaking
with beating hearts.
We made them into lies,
lies we believe tell the truth.
And we lie to each other.
And we lie to our students.
And we lie to ourselves.
And we don't know we're doing it.

Carl Rogers is not real –
not the Rogers you imagine
not the Rogers I imagine.
Of course the man was real.
He once lived
and breathed
and had a beating heart
and wrote words that soar
over space and time.
His words found their way to me.

His words found their way
into me.
His words inspire me
they live new life in me
they grow in me.
And that
is real.

My respect for how you see yourself
is real.
My respect for how you define yourself
is real.
My respect for how you express yourself
is real.
My respect for your own power
is real.
You know when you experience respect.
Your experience of that respect
is real.
Your knowledge of that experience
is real.

My books are not real.
I love my children.
But they are not real.
The words in them may reach you.
They may soar over space and time
and find new life in you
and grow.
The life they find
in you
is real.
But these words on a page,
they are not real.
Don't hold on to them.
Don't make them lies
by making them real.
They are not real.

I am real right now in this moment.
My voice is real
my experience is real
my beating heart is real.
You are real
your beating heart is real
your experience is real
your voice is real,
and I want to hear you
and see you.
Each of you is real.
This moment is real.
This moment between us
right now
is real.

Let's stop pretending
that anything else is real.

I'm gonna run
Viv Gordon

I'm gonna run
I'm gonna run down the stairs and out of the building
I'm gonna to run up the street and down the next street
And I'm gonna keep on running until I find the green
And I will not let anything get in my way and I will run to the
    top of the highest hill
And I will speak
And people will listen
Because what I have to say is important
And what I have to say is this
It is not just me
This is not just my story
There are thousands, millions of people just like me
Walking around in this deafening silence
Lots and lots and lots of people
Same story
Different details
Same story
Same excruciating denial
And now it's time for the world to listen
Because something has to change
This can't go on forever
So I am going to run
And I am going to speak
Because I can
And I am telling you
And you need to pay attention
You need to be part of the change
There is no cosy middle ground here
There is no neutral position
You are either running with us changing things
Or you are keeping everything the same
And you don't want to be that person
Because this is shit
This is shit that we cannot run away from

That we can only run towards
Weeping and hollering and fierce and raging
And together we're going to get through this
You and me
All of you
And all of me
Together
And that's just how it is
And that's how it's going to be

In this moment
Mitzy Sky

I am the hope and dreams of my ancestors, Maya Angelou writes
    in a poem.
I could fully embrace that now.
But in time past when I was a child, laying with my back against
    the earth, looking up at the sun, the blue sky, around
    me *awareness* of my *being*, I had no connection to that
    statement *at all*.
For once upon a time my ancestors had peace and freedom.
In those moments, that was all I had.

I bear witness that I had to experience psychiatric oppression to
    understand the oppression of slavery. In this moment, *I AM
    SO SORRY.*
I was compliant, given labels and drugs, saying, 'thank you, more
    please'.
I was not rebellious like the people who tried to free themselves
    from slavery and labeled *Drapetomania.*
Equivalent in my mind to forced psychiatry.
People who knew of the injustice and fought for human rights
    and freedom.
Instead, shame and guilt consumed me, and my fear was used
    against me.
I blamed myself, as the oppressor judged and labeled me.
Colluding with my torturers, saying something was wrong with
    me.
Instead of asking *what happened to me, causing me mental slavery.*

Desperate for the 'American Dream' shown on TV of Mercedes
    Benz and white picket fences, I accepted the *help.*
Agreeing with the labels caused me to judge myself the same and
    I became my worst enemy.
I did not teach myself this hate towards me, but only I could
    remember freedom and free myself.
It is no excuse to stay unconscious and not learn and grow.
The ignorance I thought was bliss almost left me lifeless.
Used for someone else to profit from my *suffering.*

Drugged but they called it medicated.

Labeled but they called it diagnoses.

Hindered but they called it helping.

Having peace and freedom again in this lifetime is no small thing.

Having peace and freedom again in this lifetime meant
recognising the pain within.

Having peace and freedom... Peace and freedom. Peace and
freedom meant feeling every emotion, perhaps looked like
'sin' – *sometimes it did.*

Having peace and freedom again in this lifetime, means
forgiveness and letting love win.

I beg you to Remember Freedom

As the first existence on this planet called Earth.

In this moment of time my grandma is getting beat.

Unable to go to school, not learning how to read.

In this moment my grandmother is reciting Bible verses to me.

Every night before I lay my head down to sleep... *I am grateful
for her great memory.*

In this moment my mother is being raped by her brother.

And threatened to be killed by him, when she spoke up, asking
him to stop raping their little sister.

In this moment my mother is beating me with electric cords
and rubber hoses, telling me, I am black and ugly like my
father... *I believe her.*

In this moment I see my mother, she is a little girl and she hasn't
healed.

She feels pain... She wants to feel love... She hurts, so she wants
to hurt me.

In this moment my peace is a threat to her. My questioning her
inadequacies is a threat to her.

In this moment I know she only did to me what was done to her.

In this moment I work hard for awareness.

My suffering was never a brain disease that any pill could heal.

In this moment my mind is wrapped up in the hurt and pain,
thinking of the past and dreaming of the future that never
would come.

It's the soul that needed the surgery, Beyoncé sings in a song.

The time is always *NOW*.

In this moment I buy my mother dinner and sit and share life with her.

She is proud of her grandkids.

In this moment my father has all he needs and more from his parents but being taught he is less than by his grandfather.

Great granddad said, leave the mangoes on the ground let them rot.

My dad was a hungry belly little tot.

A wealthy man with a fancy car once treated him nicely.

The effects of better-than still lingered greatly.

My father wished to be a big-shot man and drive big cars, lots of money and nice clothes.

In this moment my father is manipulating his child.

He says, you should make sure people always like you.

In this moment he is touching me… I want him to love me.

In this moment I have cried many tears, hated myself, think that I would have been better off dead.

Feelings of shame and guilt consumed me.

In this moment my tiny hand is holding his as we walk in the sunshine… *Confidence is mine!*

In this moment, I forgive him.

In this moment I am telling what has happened to me.

In this moment family members won't speak to me.

In this moment it doesn't matter if anyone likes me… *Keeping secrets would cause my soul to die.*

In this moment I have children that I desire to love unconditionally.

Instead I've come to expect them to live for me while I *die slowly*.

I've created great burdens for them to carry by dumping my suffering and my sorrows on them.

In this moment my child tells me that he sits at the closed window in the dark with the curtains drawn. He has watched my loneliness engulfed me. He wants to reach me.

He tells jokes to make me laugh.

He sees me sad and asks, 'Mommy will you cry today?'

I don't know how to reach him because I can't reach me. *I am numb on psychotropic drugs.*

In this moment I accept a diagnosis for my child.
I look to those with titles in their professional roles to tell me what his human experience means.
I don't push him to study hard or read a book.
TV has taken over our time to share, talk, learn together or even cook.
Fast food has become our constant remedy to comfort what cannot be comforted.
A hole in the space that should be a mother's and a father's love.

In this moment my child wishes me to see her.
Mommy look, I am standing at the edge of the train track, come and catch me before I fall.
Mommy look, why can't you see me, don't you love me at all?
Yes, my love, I see you, but I can't see me. *In this moment I am stuck.*
You try to rise above but my words of failure and defeat keep repeating… repeating… repeating.
I tell you that you are the eagle and there is no bottle, you could soar as high as you want to fly.
In this moment you are my child and I want freedom for you.
Baby girl, can't you see, I went to ask for help, I dreamt of a better life for you and me.
But accepting the labels left me like a monkey with my hand under the glass reaching for the peanut, *stuck… Completely forgetting my greatness.*
What was happening in my mind?
Shame, blame, disgust, fear, pain, better than, less than, anger, regret, lacking… burdens.
I wanted to love you, I wanted to love myself, but I kept judging, comparing and competing.
In this moment, I don't know what love is, *for if it is never received how could it be given?*

In this moment all of us are living in this vulnerable world.
I've learned to respect other's life experiences and take risks to live my own.

Strangers have become friends that support me and lift me up.
Yesterday is gone… Tomorrow not here yet… And the present moment is beautiful.

In this moment love has returned.
Who does it profit to call myself names?
In this moment it made me feel validated that I wasn't bad for the things I couldn't control, that happened to me.
But then the label took away the expectations for me to live up to my best human potential.
What that means for me.

In this moment I started to dream again.
I see myself running as fast as I can again.
I start learning about myself again.
In this moment others can't see me… so I have to see myself again.
In this moment I ask the question, *who says I'm well?*
In this moment I lost trust in myself and I ask, *how do I know I'm well?*
In this moment I am consciously unlearning all the things I unconsciously learned,
And I know that I decide Who I Am.

In this moment learning to let go as quickly as possible has given me strength to forgive and move forward, not expecting perfectionism.
In this moment there *IS*… forgiveness.
I've gained *awareness*… I found myself worthy… In this moment I find you worthy.
I believe we are all worthy.

In this moment I want a mother and a father.
I imagined it meant unconditional love.
In this moment I have support, love, connection and belonging.
The suffering has brought clarity.
It's not about the *pretty*, it's about the *presence*.
I work to stop letting 'pain be motivation'.
I am from the kidnapped people sold into chattel slavery; their strength used to build nations.

I'm from the people who held their children up to the sky saying, 'There is nothing greater than you under the sun.'
I'm the one because of *internalized oppression* forgot how to have fun.
In this moment I'm rolling down hills, walking barefoot in the streams and catching butterflies.
I am the hopes and the dreams of my ancestors.
In this moment I have peace.
In this moment I am *free*. In this moment I'm just me.

Empire
Jo McFarlane

The DSM is getting bigger,
more audacious
in its claims
Colonising difference
in its patriarchal sweep

Every human trait a species
of disorder to be subjugated
to the will of doctors
Nothing that we say or do
is normal anymore

In whose interests are the
territories of the mind enslaved?
Why give up our protest and dissent –
the lush green spaces we inhabit
they call madness?

A foreign power
alien and threatening encroaches
every corner of the globe
Sanitising us
with deference and complicity

That we too may be its agents
as we silently retreat
into the diagnostic ghettoes
where the natives are allowed
to freely roam

'Empire' was first published in A Tough Nut to Crack *(2017)*

Note: The DSM is *The Diagnostic and Statistical Manual of Mental Disorders*, published by the American Psychiatric Association, which lists all the diagnoses used in Western psychiatry.

Your chemical embrace

James Moore

I keep digging
But just getting deeper
I keep climbing
But the mountain gets steeper
And I question myself
Every single day
Can't find solace
In things I used to love
Can't deal with
Daily push and shove
Like I'm below ground
Frightened of what's above
Didn't know I was in trouble
When I fell into
Your chemical embrace
But now I can see
When is all said and done
You're a chemical disgrace
Diagnosis made me lost
Treatment made me sick
And I've only got myself to blame
You played your mind trick
Now all I feel is shame
Every single day
I'm dependent, lost and confused
The world turns but I am still
Lost the fight, lost the will
I'm as empty and hollow
As the promises
You made to me
Didn't know I was in trouble
When I fell into
Your chemical embrace
But now I can see
When is all said and done

You're a chemical disgrace
Haven't even got the strength
To be angry anymore
Feel so hollow
Deep in my core
You're not a chemical solution
But a toxic execution

First published on www.madinamerica.com and
www.madintheuk.com (14 July, 2018)

The object of my hate
Anonymous

I received this poem with the message below via email. I wanted
to include it here. I think it is important. *Jo Watson*
'I just wanted to say how much I admire your work and the efforts
you make to challenge the harm that our mental health services
can do. I've worked in mental health for a number of years, on the
wards and in the community. I put this poem together based on a
number of my previous experiences that I'm now ashamed of. Feel
free to make use of it in any way you see fit.'

It begins when the skin is opened
and angry and red.
And the pain. The pain and the weight,
The worthless hopeless state I'm in.
It's crushing
The accusatory crimson pool.
I wasn't there. I didn't care.
The long lacerations flog me. Worthless, hopeless and in pain.
This pitiful state.
It's easier to hate.

I tell them how to feel,
that their voices, they aren't real, and the cuts that they don't
mention are them just seeking attention. Their requests for
medication
are all pure manipulation.
Anything that slows discharge,
I write down as sabotage

... and when they know that I don't like them, When they say
'please someone else,' When they ask to see the kind one
When they say that I can't help – then,

I tell them that they're splitting
And I tell them I can see
That everything they think and do and feel is typical 'PD'

There are holes inside of me. An emptiness, I fill
Using skill and altruism
I make people better

It shows that I am good
and I don't know what to do.

You're taking away
What stops me being you.

And I hate that I can't help you. And I hate the way I feel
And I hate how much I hate
And just how hard it is to deal

With how my cruelty protects me
Means I somehow still respect me
I project my shit and fling it
So I still feel the correct me.
But I know. I know. I go and shut
The nursing station door. No more Interaction. Silent, solemn
        contemplation.

I just want the shift to end. Alone
I wait.
The object of my hate.

Battle weary
Sally Fox

Is everything to be a battle?
A fight for the right to be heard
with dignity and respect
after a diagnosis that renders you all but dead
Despite your best efforts
to comply with treatments
that challenge you to change...
Damned if you do
Damned if you don't
Because the land lies the same.
And the same lies regurgitate
And designate you unfit for human compassion.
My armour is heavy, my resistance is low
I've run out of places to go
My choices are diminishing, I am tired and finishing with services
        that haven't served me well
That have kept me in this hell and told me it's all my own doing
Stigma and stones are thrown at my being
I am the enemy and nobody is seeing me as I fall on my sword
They label me non-compliant, manipulative, attention-seeking
My resolve is weakening
I become what's expected of me
A self-fulfilling prophecy
A statistician's legacy
A suicide
A victim
And still you blame me.

First published in Stigma and Stones *(3rd ed) (2018).*

Dignity cannot be taken four times a day
Dolly Sen

Being labelled, pathologised and medicated, I cannot claim my
    mind for myself
I cannot claim my life for myself
So how can I even have dignity?
Medicine does not heal but seals the scream
Is that dignity?
Dignity is never in the side effects.
Weight gain – my arse is getting bigger than my dreams. Too
    tired to reach for the day, let alone the sun.
Try having sex without coming – dignity?

Love with a lot of going – dignity?
A journey of a thousand miles starts with a single step, but try it
    with a largactyl shuffle.
Constipation does not feel like dignity
How can I sing the song of dignity, drooling?
I would walk away with my head held high, but am too tired, too
    alone, too despised.
But let's put aside the pills for a moment.
Is dignity in the waiting room?
Is it in the set of eyes that sees you as a sickness?
How much does dignity cost exactly? It's not in our budget this
    year. It's not in the economic case.
Dignity is not in the control and restraint, face down, begging
    to breathe. It was not in the staggered silence of my
    'community care'.
It is not in the 'burden of care' phrase.
I am still waiting for my appointment with dignity.
Dignity means not begging for my identity, my dreams, it means
    not begging to be heard, to be cared for.
Dignity means honouring the person, but not being hated will
    do. Dignity cannot be taken four times a day.
And shouldn't be bitter pills to swallow...

Don't blame the canaries

Matthew Morris

In the coal mines they used canaries to warn of toxic threat
Saving many lives the miners owed the birds a debt
When they knew the atmosphere was dangerous the miners could
    survive
It was the birds who were suffering to keep the men alive

In our services and in society there is a narrative that denies
The reality of people's suffering we are stifling the cries
We are hiding from the truth and we are blaming the canaries
We need to protect them now so could you listen to them, please?

Don't blame the canaries for the choking chemicals they breathe
For struggling in environments where they were never supposed
    to be
Don't blame the canaries as they writhe and contort with pain
They have experienced untold traumas, then are told that they're
    insane

Don't blame the canaries for the places they were born
For the colour of their feathers or the fact that they are poor
Don't blame the canaries for the contaminated air that surrounds
It is a climate that we created, inequality abounds

Don't blame the canaries who don't serenade or sing
Some pain has no words, some songs take time to bring
Don't blame the canaries, the ones who we employ to care
For breaching and missing targets that are unachievable and unfair

There is a climate crisis and an urgent war to wage
Not about our planet warming but one of hidden rage
The anger of injustice, the screams of mental pain
The blatant abuse of power creates a bitter acid rain
A toxic landscape of human suffering and feelings of distress
Mountains of rejection, oceans of fear and stress

Just as we are all the problem, we are also the only hope
We can resolve the situation, we can overcome and cope

We can acknowledge the true issues that create the pain we feel
We can stop blaming the canaries and find a way to heal

Not by diagnosing a disorder or treating with psychoactive pills
But accepting we are all canaries and adopting more compassionate
    drills
Being kind and understanding, by listening and then listening
    some more
Being curious and compassionate, oh, and then listening some more

Not by blaming the canaries for the injustice that has been
For the pain that others inflicted, for their scars, some hidden
    others seen
Not by blaming the canaries when they can't tolerate our help
They are not treatment resistant, their resistance is to power, its
    toxic arrogance smelt

Not by Mental Health Awareness or ridiculous First Aid
For they will only multiply the canaries, making us all jump into
    their cage
Instead of addressing the issues they medicalise who we are
They deny the mess around us, signposting to other canaries who
    don't know that is who they are

If you are a canary we must all apologise, your suffering is not
    your fault we must all accept the blame
Whether directly or indirectly we have all fanned a noxious flame
If you are a canary we must release you from your cage
So you can spread your wings and fly to safety, somewhere to assuage

If you are a canary your story must be heard
You must sing your song and celebrate, your survival cannot be
    deterred
Your plumage is magnificent whatever colour you are
Your sensitivity can save the rest of us, you can be our guiding star

Of course we are all canaries in different aviaries
We're a very strange kind of animal, a contrary, bizarre species
We have it within us to be destructive cruel and aloof
But also kind and loving and all around there's proof

So please don't blame the canaries for our failure to engage
And don't wait for their extinction or until we are all sitting in
    their cage
A revolution has started and you are all invited to join in
Although you are already part of it and nobody's told you to begin
Together we can listen to our hearts and let them inform our heads
Fighting for our feelings to be seen as perfect, not symptoms to
    be dread
We can tear down ideas of illness that are built on a dangerous air
Of inaccuracy and a power grab that is around us everywhere
So let us all go forward with courage and always be aware
That if we listen to our canaries we cannot fail to get there

A million conversations about 'ECT'
Jo Watson

'It works' – they say
'what's not to like?
It helps a broken brain
Succeeds where other stuff has failed
Makes people less insane

'Oh, also – it's a last resort
Like, it's not the first idea
By this point they've tried everything
Long lists of panaceas...

'All psychiatry's offerings
Mostly every pill
But the brain is proper broken, see
A severe type of ill!

'OK, there's no real evidence
Don't be put off by this
The proof is they are still alive
And that we can't dismiss!'

'So, let me get this right' – I say
'I want to understand
You think that shocking someone's brain
Should definitely not be banned?

'And despite the lack of evidence
You're happy it's a choice
Even though what most have heard
Is a mainstream biased voice...

'Telling them of brain disease
And conditions without cure
Explaining that it's all medical
Like this will reassure?

''cause if I was told that theory
It would evoke a deep despair

I'd feel trapped inside my brokenness
Without a hope or prayer

'To the point where I might too
Consider "ECT"
Desperation will try most things
I'm sure you would agree?

'For many in this torment
Never had a real choice
To understand stuff differently
To hear an inner voice...

'That just might tell them stories
Of core hurts and pain
And give some sense and meaning
To potentially explain...

'Their life-long daily struggle
To function, to exist
Compounded by the hopelessness
Of illness narratives'

'Nah', they say, 'it's not like that
Bad stuff is not the thing
This is flawed biology
It's chemicals, it's genes.'

So I had to leave it there then
To pick up another day
There was no sign of movement
There was nothing I could say

But while this is accepted
And presented as the facts
In schools, in films, on twitter
It conveniently detracts...

From all the things that happen
All the social ills
And from any real acknowledgement
That it's unheard pain that kills

**Other than personality disorder, what term could you use
to describe these people?**
Clare Shaw

These people are Arctic Terns
who launch their tiny weight into the wind.
Their problem is winter,

their problem is weather; they avoid storms
by taking the largest detours to find land
and they are abundant.

These people fly between poles
and they sleep on the wing – they spiral,
their endurance is legendary.

They will bite your head
if they have to: they will draw blood.
They sing a high song of alarm

and they know two summers;
They have been studied and trapped
and tracked in their journeys,

these people are remarkable –
they have magnets inside their heads
and they go where they have to.

They know the glow of the snow
on the water, the sea as a glimmer,
the mountains as blades in the sky.

And they are the subject of various papers.
And life is harsh, and days are endless.

Labels

Jacky Power

I am more than just a label that you try to pin on me.
My behaviour will betray me if that is all you see.
You can try to reduce my being – call out addiction or OCD
Dehumanise, pathologise, compartmentalising me.
I'm not a 'wash at 30' or 'fat content 3%'.
No, labels are for objects – not breathing sentients.
I'm a human whose emotional life's gone slightly out of whack.
Help me see my strengths and virtues so I can find my own way
    back
To the me I know that's in there when I peel away the pain.
I'm due my humanness – like you.
Underneath we're all the same.

Text book
Dr Peter Gordon

TEXT book.
Evidence contained within
is empirical and 'disinterested'
providing science at its most objective.

TEXT book.
Has a 'target on its back [cover]' –
because 'real' science needs defending!

TEXT book.
Provides all the evidence you may need
whilst ignoring all that matters in between.

TEXT book.
Where evidence is
divided,
numbered,
labelled,
categorised.

TEXT book.
I am not there.
Are you?

Manipulation
Jo McFarlane

I've been a puppet of psychiatry
for 27 years
Complicit cos it suited me
to have a hand shoved up my rear

I can't claim blissful ignorance;
that the drugs weren't doing me harm
So, cognitively dissonanced,
I let them twist my arm

But why collude so gratefully,
convincing them for sure…?
And thus let them complacently
take credit for a cure

It was expedient to see myself as sick,
and they – my blessed saviours
By compensating childhood deficit
their intervention was a favour

And who can blame me for regressing
when the opportunity was there?
My naïve attempt at second-guessing
pharmacology for care

Medication numbed me
from the pain I was avoiding
It soothed me like a dummy
Now the sedative I'm hoarding

No one asked me categorically
Do you want to take this pill?
But by agreeing allegorically
my acquiescence said *I will*

If I had refused, no doubt
the pain would have receded

If they'd let me scream and shout
They'd know that understanding's what I needed

But it suited them to keep me docile
so that they could pull my strings
And now my reason for withdrawal:
So that I can find my wings

'Manipulation' was first published in A Tough Nut to Crack *(2017)*

I am a storm

Erin Stevens

This poem was inspired by the impact of intergenerational iatrogenic harm.

I am a blue-black raincloud,
A shroud of ashen hue
Unravelling like velvet
And enveloping the view.
My mind is growing pressure,
The accelerating breeze,
The scattering of songbirds
And the dancing of the trees.
My thoughts are fading shadows
On a newly darkened beach
The vaguest hint of sunshine
Swiftly rolling out of reach.
My words are growling thunder
Rising up to fearsome claps
Electric sparks connect the clouds
With every fired synapse.
My emotions are a downpour
Lashing wildly to the floor.
Suspended in oppressive clouds
Till they can hold no more.
My body is the battered land
Left reeling in its wake
Rebuilding and restoring calm
With every breath I take.

First published on www.adisorder4everyone.com (September, 2019)

What if psychiatry has got it all wrong?
Dr Jessica Taylor

What if psychiatry has got it all wrong and it was oppressing and
abusing women all along?
What if women have been systematically medicated so they never
have their experience of trauma validated?

What if girls are convinced they are mentally ill so they never
realise their own talent and skill?
What if the purpose of publicly burning the witches was so we
never followed the footsteps of our feminist sisters?

What if they locked up women who were abused by men so they
never had to listen when he raped someone again?
What if the asylums were filled to the rafters with lesbians who
never dreamt of the hetero-ever-after?

What if the young girls made pregnant by Dad were locked up
for decades and labelled as mad?
What if women were put on untested pills by a doctor who
ignored trauma and wrote she was mentally ill?

What if teen girls are removed and locked up, alone because the
psychiatrist says it's false memory syndrome?
What if women and girls have their disclosures contested so their
abusers and rapists are never arrested?

What if ECT and its numbness and pain is causing irreparable
damage to the brain?
What if borderline personality disorder isn't even real and it was
created simply to pathologise the way women feel?

What if millions of women are taking two pills a day for a
disorder they've been told will never go away?
What if psychiatry has got it all wrong and women and girls have
been telling the truth all along?

Revenge of the crazy wimmin
Leah Ida Harris

the man's always had a plan
to slow down the velocity of woman's journeys
to lower the volume of woman's voices
saying hush now honey be calm be still
the powers that be saying
there's an appropriate level for your grief and
there's a healthy range for your rage
and when woman exceeds
the emotional speed limit
society put on the brakes

and the more things change
the more they stay
the same
they using the same tactics
but they just change the names

back in the middle ages
they burned unruly women at the stake
and out of the ashes of their bones and flesh
rose the Enlightenment and Reason fresh
and the white men declared
there's no such thing as witches
they're just crazy psycho-bitches
but we certainly can't let them run free
lock 'em up and throw away the key

cause there's nothing scarier than a woman mad and/or
aware of her own magic
tragic how much violence is done
in the name of science
to ensure our silence

in Victorian times they located suffering in our uterus
in the blood in the soft internal organs
took our pain our righteous rage

they called it "hysteria"
and then Dr. Freud ignored women's horror stories
herstories of abuse and rape and
took a justified hatred of the penis and called it
envy (he sold more books that way)

what they call paranoia
we call reality hitting us hard
when we name the forces all around
conspiring to keep us down
when we deny the diagnoses of our masters
when we refuse to be sick, defective, diseased, disordered, disturbed

when we dare to proclaim our humanity
when we accuse THEM of insanity
they call it "lack of insight"
into our condition

but we got an insight that'll blind you

we know something about our conditions
and how we came to be confined:
our husbands our kids they wanted our house our money
yeah it's kinda funny how it goes down
we were visionaries who shared our visions with the wrong people
we were too poor too butch too ugly too far-gone on the mean
        streets
we seen shit nobody should ever have to see
we got raped got beat got tortured by strangers and
the ones who claimed to love us
and when life comes apart at the seams
when the castles of our dreams implode
we chase the needle in search of the next high
put on a skirt, fuck who we have to just to get by
and when our demons chase us till
we break up
from the pure exhaustion of being alive
and you're lucky if you survive, honey
yeah, you're lucky if you survive

first: there's a diagnosis for every tragedy
then they sign the forms lock us up put us in solitary
shame us call us names tell us we won't amount to nothing
wrestle us down to the ground with their male arms
"treat" us--like shit--tie us up naked bruised and shaking
dope us up with their drugs so we can't stand
can't write can paint can't think can't speak
wrap us in white sheets (when we ain't dead yet)
take our babies from us
lobotomize us sterilize us electroshock us
rape us kill us
saying this is for your own good
this is for your own good
this is for
your own good

this is for all the mamas daughters sisters lovers friends
who ended up behind bars
and this is for every woman who died alone
in a locked cell
this is for every woman who's ever survived hell
and emerged to tell the tale to her sisters

our voices thick with saliva and blood speaking
truth my sisters truth my fellow witches unreasonable women

yes we are "acting out"
cackling at the scourge of normalcy
as defined by the men waging endless war a la 1984
we diagnose them with "mass destruction disorder"
and write out a prescription for the maximum dose of
justice
and out on the horizon
gather the storm-clouds of our retaliation
in a collective conflagration
we are rising up
picking up the scattered pieces of what shattered
building and birthing out new visions for the generations to come
with our rage of the ages

the force of our breath
we are shaking off death
and taking in life

the crazy wimmin gonna have the last laugh someday
and it's gonna be
loud

First published in Word Warriors: women leaders in the spoken
word revolution *(Seal Press, 2007)*

Watching the sun rise from her chair
Ruth E. Dixon

An empty flat and still I am,
Kitchen cupboards lined with spam,
She will not see me waiting there,
To watch the sun rise from her chair.

My easing limbs as thoughts uncrease,
The glimmers of eventual peace,
Her apron rests upon the door,
To meet last night, to meet once more?

The promise brought with golden blaze,
Of tumbling years, unfolding days,
And still I am and there I sit,
To soak up every little bit.

Her chair wraps me in honeycomb,
But I have wilderness to roam,
And miles to go before I'm home,
And miles to go before I'm home.

Everything you have ever lost
Joelle Taylor

(i)

everything you have ever lost is in here.

How the lines on your face were written
how you could not afford your own face

how your face was a battlefield, deserted;
a war between parents

how your pockets were tunnels and you were lost in them
how no one came even though you called all night

how your call was the sound of something small breaking
how your teeth were tower blocks in which only white ghosts
        lived

how your skin was a lost birth certificate
how your birth certificate was proof of your death

how they stole your smile to store on a high supermarket shelf
how the industry unmade you

how your tongue was a conveyor belt
and you could not make the words fast enough

how your soul was kept well-fed in a zoo
how the zoo was a library of lost souls

how the souls stared unblinking from glass enclosures
how the glass was etched with the hieroglyphics of rage

How you made an origami figure of a small boy staring
how some boys cry with their fists

How some boys hang themselves
from the thin edge of their smiles

how they told you that white
was the colour that contained all others

how your skin became a colour that contained you
how skin becomes insignia

how they sold black back to you
at inflated prices
how rainbows are portents. how rainbows are borders.

how you travelled to the other side of the rainbow
and met a stranger travelling back the way you had come

how the stranger looked like you
how you are a stranger

how your ancestors will be born after you

(ii)

how they spat at you and the saliva became a sea
and you sailed easily across it to the other side of your heart

how your heart was a tectonic plate
how your heart rubbed

how it drifted apart
how other people set up home on the opposite side of your heart
    to you

how they sent smoke signals
how you answered

how your words turned to ash and blew away
how your voice was thin ice you were scared to walk across

how silence was a song your enemy taught you
how the last bus home took you to another man's city

how home keeps moving
how you knocked on the door of your home and a stranger
    answered

how your streets were gentrified
how you were forced out of your own mouth

how your father lives in your face
and nowhere else

How you were raped by a high court judge
how judges' wigs were mushroom clouds floating over the
        horizon

How your dreams were trained to walk in tight circles
how your dreams were dogs

How you named your dog after the first woman you beat
how you beat her to get all the prayers out

How you beat her, your bright piñata
so you could build a house of sweets

How you learned to walk on women
how women learned to smile at you

How their smiles were tightropes
how their smiles were cut throats

How you understood the language of the sea
and why it keeps returning

How your father was a bomb
and your mother rich in minerals

How smoke rises from mill town chimneys
and you recognise its face.

how you were dead
how you were dead
and death brought you flowers and you said thank you but you
        meant fuck you
how death waited outside all night

How pebbles against windows sound like Aleppo
how your mouth was a tornado that gathered the whole town to
        it –

everything you have ever lost is in here.

When you could have let love sat beside you on a broken
backed sofa and change the channels.
when one hand was all that was required.

When if you had placed your palm prints beside each other
you might have found they made an atlas that could lead you out
        of here.

when love might have woken you.
When you might have fallen.

and through falling uncovered the archaeology of your wings.
when after the grey apocalypse that no one else noticed

you might have realised that trees hold hands beneath the earth;
when you learned to hold hands beneath the earth.
Everything you have ever lost is in here.

Here is the music of your brother breathing
Here is the shape of your mother

Here is the shadow that abandoned you
Here is your unfound song

Here is the legend of your lost tongue
Here are your teeth. Your brittle. Your bone.

Everything you have ever lost is in here

and it is waiting
to come home.

First published in Songs My Enemy Taught Me
(Out-Spoken Press, 2017)

Trauma-reducing not trauma-inducing
Dr Karen Treisman

Trauma, oppression, privilege, and social injustice are the
    elephants in the room,

Their impact and intersectionality can colour one's kaleidoscope
    from womb to their tomb,

To see the whole person, their story, their world, and to not
    reduce them to a label,

And to magnify, celebrate, and learn from people's survivorship,
    strengths, resources and what they bring to the table,

As Alexander den Heijer says if a flower doesn't bloom fix the
    environment in which in grows not the flower,

We need to widen our lens to incorporate inequality, oppression,
    poverty, discrimination, and abuse of power,

Cultural humility is needed with a commitment to lifelong
    learning and critical evaluation,

Through proactive responsiveness and active knowledge seeking
    and education,

Where systems are designed and structured to be healthy and
    reflective; instead of reactive and trauma inducing,

We need our systems to be brick parents who work towards and
    are committed to be trauma reducing,

Instead of fragmented and disconnected systems they should
    prioritise humanity and mutuality,

Having traumatised systems in survival modes themselves – now
    that is insanity,

Systems which value human rights and do everything that they
    can to ensure protection,

Ones which focus on reparative relationships which are
    committed to a healing connection,

We need to see the layers and the richness throughout people's
inner and outer Russian dolls,

To notice, respect, and honour the multi-layered reasons for
some of those painful holes,

And to see trauma as the piercing force it can be which can
wound and hurt the soul,

The responses from traumatised services can be retriggering,
harmful, and catapult people down a memory time hole,

Trauma is the ultimate boundary violation and betrayal of trust,

This is someone's story, someone's truth, not just a statistic in a
policy collecting dust,

We can't take down fences until we honour why they developed
and why they needed to be there,

There is a lot to be said about increasing safety, trust, openness,
and truly showing that you care,

We can promote, market, use the buzzwords, and try to talk the
talk,

But it's so much more than that, it's how we truly and
meaningfully walk the walk,

We need to humanise services and put relationships and
connections at the heart,

Infusing the values of curiosity, compassion, humanity, and
empathy would be an amazing start,

Developmental and relational trauma require developmental and
relational repair,

And our communities and our systems need to not marinate and
soak us in a suffocating traumatic fog and air,

To see behaviours as survival needs and signals rather than as a
label, a deficit, or a flaw,

To see the whole person behind the behaviour, who has the potential to grow and soar,

If the behaviour had a voice what would it say,

How can we see and appreciate the patchwork of colours and all the shades of grey?

As Maya Angelou said, People will forget what you do and forget what you say but they will remember how you make them feel,

After all, it's not about othering, it's about being human, being kind, having humility, and being real,

We all need to feel valued, noticed, heard, listened to, and seen,

And to feel that we are the author of our own stories and the navigator of where we have been,

The position has shifted from what is wrong with you, to what has happened to you,

To one which sees a person within their wider context and all which they have lived through,

And again, it is not what is the matter with you but what matters to you,

The puzzle pieces and the golden thread of identity that answers the who,

It's not about labelling, fitting people into boxes, and shaming,

It's about holding onto hope, to uniqueness, rather than splitting them and us, and blaming,

It is easy to get lost or silenced. Whose voices are neglected or missing? Whose are heard and whose are speaking?

How can we reframe and see things as attention needing rather than as attention seeking?

It's so much more than words and talking therapies, as trauma is encoded in our bodies and in our senses,

It is seeing the hurt, the pain, the moral injury behind and hidden beneath the defences, offences, and fences,

We need to find ways to connect, co-regulate, and make it safe to unveil from the shame-ridden cloak,

We need to hold, convey, and anchor on to sparkle moments, connection, and hope,

Because every moment counts and every interaction can be an intervention,

We need to make a vow to do no harm, that should be our most obvious intention,

As the African proverb says if you want to go fast go alone, if you want to go far go together,

Let's join like an orchestra of beating drums to not allow ourselves to be pushed aside like a floating feather,

Thank you for your time, your energy, your presence, and your listening ear,

I'm honoured, humbled, and privileged to be here

Unlabelled
Jo McFarlane

Today I shrugged it off
like a useless coat
whose heavy arms had
strangled me so long
and now were cut off at the seam.
Today I learnt my personality is A-ok,
I'm not malignant or dysfunctional,
I'm not the woman
you cross the street to escape.

Today I learnt the pain that's been consuming me so long
is not my fault, is not my fate,
is not my punishment for things I didn't do.
People have hurt me to the point I wear their scars,
perhaps because they couldn't help themselves,
heal themselves or love themselves.
That doesn't mean I have to hate them,
doesn't mean I have to hate myself,
doesn't mean I have to wear a coat that I've outgrown.

I'm born again of possibility.
To know that you believe in me
is reason more than I dared hope
to find myself another coat
that keeps me warm,
that suits my beautiful curves,
that we've gone shopping for together
'cos I couldn't be this liberated
were it not for you!

'Unlabelled' was first published in Coming Up for Air *(2011)*

I do not believe in silence

Clare Shaw

Because, tonight –
however I try – I cannot get downstairs
without waking my daughter
I do not believe in silence.

Because of the Warboys enquiry,
because of the one hundred-plus women he raped –
because of the policeman defending the findings
unable to utter the word –
'this (herrrrm) crime, this (ahem)
assault, this category (cough)
of offence' –
I do not believe in silence

because of the stairs and the banister's crack;
the sound of the lock
and my hand on the door – the fifty-tone creak –
the magnificent echo of light-switch and click –
I do not believe in silence.

Because of Neda – and everyone's sister –
and the man who said 'Don't be afraid';
for the sake of my daughter, because of the burkha,
because of the patter of rain;
because of two hundred-thousand years of human history,
thirty-seven of them my own –
I do not believe in silence

for the sake of my arms, the wrists especially.
With respect to my legs
and my belly and chest
and the comfort long due to my throat

because of nightclubs at one am
and shouts in the street and feet in pursuit
and shops that don't shut;
because of sirens and the dealers downstairs;

because of Levi and Akhmatova;
because of the blue-lipped prisoner;
the itch and the scratch of my pen;

I believe in the word.
I believe in the scrabble of claws
on uncarpeted floors.
I believe in my daughter's complaints.
I believe in the violin, the E-string,
the see-sawing bow; the cello
straining its throat.

I believe in the heart and its beat
and its beep and the dance of the trace
on the screen, I believe in the volume
of colour turned up, and my blood
which was always too loud.

Because of the nights, and the sweats,
and the same rowdy thoughts;
because that one afternoon
when I nailed my own voice to the air
and because there was nobody listening
and through it all
birdsong
and the sound of cars passing –

I do not believe in silence.

First published in Head On *(Bloodaxe, 2012)*

Fuck you
T.O. Walker

Fuck You
I won't be
The right type
Of victim
I won't be the
Quiet type
Of victim
I won't fit
Neatly
Into boxes
For you to close
I am not sick
Or broken
Irreparably
Damaged
I refuse to be
Well
And recovered
Fixed
And mended
I am not
A statistic
To be counted
Or dismissed
I am more than that
I am not
One page of a book
One leaf on a tree
One voice in a crowd
I'm all the words and sounds
I am a forest of ideas
A chorus of experiences
I am not
A professional
An academic

An undercover reporter
I am not
A mother
A partner
A sister
A daughter
I am not single
But many
A multitude
Of identities
Fuck you
And your labels
Your projections
Of my stability
My strengths
My life
My capability
My everything
You don't know
Who I am
You can't see
Past your assumptions
Your agenda and vendetta
Your arrogant
Hypocrisy
You're blinded by
desire to silence
But the cat's out the bag
You cannot keep me
Quiet
Until the cows come home
That day has ended
And a change has begun

I'm with her

Jo Watson

This poem was written for International Women's Day 2016 and has been a part of the AD4E events since they started in October of the same year.

It was inspired by Eleanor Longden's Ted talk, *The Voices In My Head*, in which she tells her story of being 'diagnosed, drugged and discarded' and shares the powerful quote originally coined by Dr Vincent Felitti: 'The main question in psychiatry shouldn't be "What's wrong with you?" It should be "What happened to you?"'

And I'm with her
like not 'on the fence'
'cause surely our mental health *is*
linked to experience
so often a direct consequence
of trauma, of oppression
and I don't know about you
but I'm getting the impression
that we've been being tricked
like – really – good and proper
into feeling, believing
that these problems
tell us – about *us* – about who we are
rather than what it was
that actually carved the scar

you see, we're fooled into thinking
it's about biology, physiology
intrinsic to identity
they tell us that it's in our genes
instead of being in the scenes of what happened to us
that play out on repeat sometimes
you know – the ones we don't mention too much.

Our great grandmothers
look – some of
our great grandmothers were incarcerated, locked away,
for years and years
left to decay
sometimes shackled in metal vices
whilst slices of their brains
were cut out
to 'exorcise' the threat
and yes this meant
they sometimes
would forget the horrors
but it also meant
that sometimes, they would forget their names

Our grandmothers
I guess it won't come as a big surprise
that large numbers of our grandmothers were tranquillised,
pretty much sedated
and this equated to a kind of half-life
often, for their entire life.
And when this didn't quite sort them out (make them sane)
they may well have been strapped down
whilst electricity was shot inside their brain

Our mothers
lots of our mothers were
flooded with old school anti-depressants
given unnecessary womb extractions
and had reactions
to instant hormones which (for some)
meant a detour
around that mid-life rite of passage
that may have brought them home

And as for our sisters, as for ourselves
well, we are labelled and medicated,
disorders allocated – often accumulated
'cause there's no shortage of diagnostic criteria

to explain any deliria
or otherwise
honestly – you'd be surprised,
there's a disorder for everyone
it's true
there's a disorder for everyone
what? *you* haven't been diagnosed yet?
well, you just haven't been
in the wrong place
saying the wrong things
to the wrong people
at the wrong time
arbitrary luck, nothing else
'cause I promise –
there *is* a disorder for everyone

they're in the book
(the *DSM-5*)
the place from where they all derive
hundreds of them
all squashed in – all planned
as supply and demand doesn't work too well
without the demand bit
so our 'disorder' has to fit
we need the pills to cure it
cure us, be our defence
chemical compounds of modern science
that conveniently turn off
or tone down
our emotions, our feelings
whilst pharmaceuticals profit so much
they're a-wheeling and a-dealing
with governments – dictating policy
is it not an atrocity?
that drug companies have *any* say
in the big decisions of the day?

I know, I get it – I'm ranting now,
but here's the thing...

subtly, hidden away
underneath the anti-stigma shiny-surfaced campaigns of the day
of 'mental health awareness raising'
that are so good at
glazing over the point
over the pain
we find more of the same
hidden away is more of the same
and excuse the pun
but this is sending me insane!

'cause now, even the good ones
are having a try,
you know,
the likes of Ruby Wax
and good old Stephen Fry
sadly still perpetuating the same old toxic lies
and generally doing a great job
of using celebrity status to pathologise
so we all get to believing that
it *is* about us
they say 'mental health is like physical health!'
and alongside that (invariably)
a belief that it's part of identity
so part of me – the heart of me
that's not going away
it's here to stay
needs to be managed
contained,
needs to be chemically explained.

so we really need a 'Rethink'
and it's definitely 'Time to Change'
because otherwise precisely nothing is being rearranged
and we'll see a continuation
of the same old, same old shit
convenient, disempowering,
medical-model-rhetoric
we'll see confusion, delusion – collusion with social control

and where the hell in all of this is oppression's role?
trauma's role?
it's not getting a look in
let alone being explored
so all of our stories join those the millions of others
that have been conveniently ignored
'cause trauma can't be relevant
it's too much of a threat
to the general scheme of things
instead we should forget
forget about what's happened, and put it down to genes
to chemical chaos, predispositions, the biological machine.

you know,
Eleanor Longden – she wasn't ever asked
about what had happened to her
or any of her past
they just said she had an illness
a kind of broken brain
and that this explained the voices and the corresponding pain
so diagnosed with 'schizophrenia'
and written off as hopeless case,
and yes you may be thinking this is an absolute disgrace
but it isn't an exception
it happens every day
it's time to change the script now
and find another way.

About the contributors

Sanah Ahsan
Sanah Ahsan is a Queer Pakistani Muslim Womxn, psychologist, poet and disrupter. *The Guardian* recently described her poetry as 'an exhilarating declaration of love and an invocation to bare the soul'. Sanah won the Outspoken performance poetry prize 2019 and delivered a TedXLondon talk on 'Rewriting my story with poetry and love as a Queer Muslim'. Her work is most recently published in Nikita Gill's anthology *Slam! You're going to want to hear this*, and her poem 'Come as you are' just featured on BBC 2's *The Way Out*. She is working on her own collection to be released soon. Sanah is a clinical psychologist, and currently uses poetry in her work with homeless people. She presented a Channel 4 documentary, *Young, British and Depressed*, and worked with WOW Festival 2020 to host a sold-out session on women of colour's mental health. Her doctoral research focuses on deconstructing whiteness within clinical psychology. Sanah's creative and therapeutic work seeks to decolonise our understandings of distress and embrace each other's madness. www.sanahahsan.com

Jyl Anais
Jyl Anais is a poet and visual artist who works at the intersections of a variety of media. Her debut poetry collection, *Soft Out Spoken*, was released in 2019. Jyl's work appears in *Protectors 2: Heroes* and *Asylum* magazine, as well as on the Mad In America website, among others. She's worked in the court system as an advocate for victims of child abuse. Originally from Trinidad, she now lives in the US, where she works as a forensic medium, makes plant medicine in her home apothecary and faces the blank page. Find her at jylanais.com

Wend Badger
Wend Badger spent the first 30 years of her career in nursing, specialising in safeguarding and domestic abuse. She now works full time for a domestic abuse charity and has worked as an expert

speaker in mental capacity and consent. In her spare time, when she's not pushing for organisations to drop the disorder, she is an avid gardener and enthusiastic but distinctly average drummer. She lives in the Midlands with her non-conforming cats.

Amanda Bueno de Mesquita

Amanda is UKCP-registered systemic family psychotherapist with three decades of working with children and families, and three adult sons of her own. She has worked in CAMHS, a charity supporting families, and on the 'mental health' wards of a London hospital. She currently works in private practice at Buenotherapy.com and within an NHS hospital crisis team. Amanda discovers explanations and solutions for the numerous and frequently seemingly perplexing issues that people may present with. Her approach is always 'What may have happened to you?' and never 'What is wrong with you?'.

Dr Julie Carter

Julie Carter grew up in Sunderland and lives near Keswick in Cumbria, UK. She started her working life as a researcher in genetics before teaching science and outdoor education, then becoming a medical doctor. After a couple of decades in emergency care and general practice, she began to look more broadly for different ways of promoting health and alleviating distress. This led her to train in Human Givens, which is an evidence-based, practical approach to health, based on getting our needs met in balance, without exploiting others. Julie is a runner, a climber and an adventurer. Her experiences in all aspects of her life are the inspiration for her writing, which crosses the genres of creative non-fiction and poetry. You can find a selection of her work, including film and audio and her blog, on her website at www.mindfell.co.uk

Lydia Daisy

Lydia Daisy is a singer-songwriter, poet, performer and charity worker. Her writing has always been firmly based in human experience and feeling. Lydia believes whole heartedly that emotional distress is rooted in what we experience. She has been a strong ally of AD4E since its beginning and is a contributor to the Drop the Disorder! poetry events.

Ruth E. Dixon

Ruth E. Dixon is a performance poet and person-centred therapist from North Lincolnshire. She has several years' experience counselling adults and teenagers and has also worked in fostering and adoption, helping young people leaving care and family support. Ruth is passionate about trauma-informed care and exploring ways for a person to make meaning of their experiences without labelling. Ruth first started performing her poetry on the open mic scene in Hull and has since taken spoken-word shows to the Brighton and Edinburgh Fringe Festivals. She has also performed as part of the BBC's poetry festival *Contains Strong Language*. Ruth's first AD4E event was Liverpool in 2017 and she has been hooked ever since. Her involvement with Drop the Disorder! coincided with a time in her life when she was grieving the loss of her mother; Andrea spent nearly 50 years in psychiatric care and was diagnosed with several mental 'disorders'. Inspired by the #MeToo movement, as well as the many survivors and activists she has met through Drop the Disorder!, Ruth has used her poetry as a way of finally giving her mother a voice, as testimony to a deeply misunderstood woman. She is delighted to be part of such a progressive and uplifting movement and feels her mum would have loved it too.

Dorothy Dundas

Dorothy is a psychiatric survivor and long-time advocate for those in the mental health system. Diagnosed with 'schizophrenia' in her late teens in the 1960s in the US, she was forced to undergo 40 combined insulin coma/electroshock 'treatments' without anaesthesia. She witnessed and experienced many atrocities. Luck, determination, anger and a compassionate advocate were her friends on the road to her survival and freedom; she has been fine for more than 55 years! Through a number of public op-ed pieces in *The Boston Globe* and a poster she created from her hospital records ('Behind Locked Doors'), she has voiced her opposition to abusive psychiatric practices. Dorothy lives in the Boston area, where she raised her four lovely and amazing children.

Martha Enticott

Martha Enticott is 16 and draws on her experiences of the mental health system to create change in the ways children and young people are supported and responded to. In her spare time, Martha likes walking her dogs.

Tracey Farrell

Tracey Farrell is a truth-speaker and wildflower woman, who works as a mental health social worker in Australia. Through her words, resource creation and education, she is known as a fierce protector of children's rights, and an advocate for building trauma-informed and attachment-focused services.

Sally Fox

Sally Fox uses visual arts and the written word to explore and communicate her experience of mental distress and using services. She has performed and exhibited widely, and her work has been published in the *British Journal of Psychiatry* and several poetry anthologies. Her areas of interest include the therapeutic process and relationship, trauma and attachment, art therapy and art journaling, LGBT identities, and the effect of labelling – in particular, the 'borderline personality disorder' diagnosis. She has devised and facilitated groups and events around all these issues. She has also contributed to the training of mental health nurses and other professionals. Sally is passionate about the power of creativity in finding our authentic voice and using it to influence change. Her books include *Putting Myself in the Frame: drawing hope from art therapy* and (co-authored with Jo McFarlane) *Stigma & Stones: poems on living with a diagnosis of 'BPD'*.

Jasmine Gardosi

Jasmine Gardosi is a multiple slam champion and Birmingham Poet Laureate finalist. A previous BBC Arts Young Creative and Poet in Residence for the Shakespeare Birthplace Trust, she has appeared across BBC radio, including Radio 3's *The Verb*, and on BBC Radio 4, at Glastonbury Festival and at Tate Modern. Her commission for Standard Chartered saw her showcased globally as part of International Women's Day, and she has been featured internationally by Button Poetry, the world's largest spoken-word platform, after being awarded an Honorable Mention for Outstanding International Entry in their 2018 video contest. The sex education show she co-created with Autin Dance Theatre is in its fourth year of development and touring, and in December 2018 she completed a residency at the Royal Court Theatre, exploring gender issues. She continues to explore topics such as sex education, LGBTQ identities, gender issues and mental health through other performances and workshops. A Ledbury Poetry Festival trustee, she leads West Midlands Poets' Place, the Hippodrome Young Poets Collective and other school and community workshops. Her debut pamphlet *Hurtz* was released in May 2020. @jasminegardosi

Dr Peter Gordon

Peter Gordon studied medicine at Aberdeen University and landscape architecture at Edinburgh University. After more than 25 years as an NHS psychiatrist, Peter retired fully from medicine in January 2020. He has a number of interests, including philosophy, sociology, ethics, medical humanities, history, architecture, horticulture, ecology, design, sculpture, poetry, and filmmaking. Peter is married with two children.

Viv Gordon

Viv Gordon is a theatre maker and survivor activist. She creates arts projects that creatively articulate trauma narratives based on her lived experience as a survivor of childhood sexual abuse, connecting the personal with wider, socio-political themes and perspectives. Her work is a campaign to forge survivor voice visibility and community and agitate for change. Viv holds a deep mistrust of mental health services and describes herself as a service dodger. She finds solace and healing in creativity, creative therapies, women's groups, nature and physical activity.

Mica Gray

Mica Montana Gray is an applied research psychologist from Birmingham, UK, of African-Caribbean heritage. She has an undergraduate degree in psychology and philosophy and an MSc in cognitive neuroscience. Outside of academia, Mica is also a writer and poet and delivers creative and reflective wellbeing workshop for community organisations. Her self-published debut poetry collection, *When Daisies Talk*, explores her own lived experiences of depression and psychosis through the intersections of race, womanhood, spirituality and psychiatry. Mica has performed at AD4E events on numerous occasions.

Jackie Hagan

Jackie Hagan is a multi-award-winning writer and performer. She is a working-class, queer amputee and full-time sick person. She has performed globally and written and acted in her own work for BBC Four and BBCAmerica. She has been under the psych team for 24 years and just today was discharged. She wonders now why she stayed so long.

Kathleen Halley Angus

Kathleen Halley Angus is a human being born of a comet, shaped by the stars and on a journey back to Earth. She has pushed life to the very edge and has vowed to spend the rest of hers expressing her love for the world through art. She writes songs and spoken word and has just authored a book, *The Midnight Manifesto*, about her explorations into consciousness and the definition of mental health. She currently lives in the Northern Rivers region of New South Wales, where she grows food and surfs badly. She can often be found in her shack in the rainforest, singing loudly and quietly making plans to take over the world. She is really good at telling the truth.

Leah Ida Harris

Leah Ida Harris is a mad, non-binary queer writer and space and time traveller.

A. Hurford

Toni Hurford is an emerging poet and writer from north east England. A survivor of the mental health system, she started to write poetry when completing an MA in counselling in 2004. Toni was happy and lucky to find Survivors' Poetry, who mentored her towards a pamphlet that's become a book, *A Staff of Asklepios*, her debut collection, forthcoming with Survivors' Press. Toni blogs and publishes occasionally with Disability Arts Online and is grateful for their support and encouragement. She maintains her own blog (https://ablindcatchinthesun), where you can find further details of published work and plenty of poems.

Sue Irwin

Sue Irwin is a passionate gardener and linguist, and mum to three adult children. She is a survivor of childhood abuse as well as the UK's mental health system, where she spent 18 years as a service user. She draws on these experiences to support the training of future mental health professionals at her local university. She is a member of a local group that offers support to people withdrawing from psychiatric medication and is a contributing author to the *Drop the Disorder!* book, as well as Emerging Proud's Pocket Book *Emerging Proud Through Trauma and Abuse*, both published in 2019. Sue worked for 12 months as a paid peer support worker in the NHS and, shortly after her resignation, wrote an article in *Mental Health & Social Inclusion* explaining her reasons for leaving. Following this, she went on to work in the voluntary sector, facilitating a community peer support initiative. Sue recently successfully completed an MSc in social and therapeutic horticulture, which she hopes will assist her in supporting a local community horticultural project.

Ruth Jackson

Rooted in the north east of England, Ruth Jackson works mostly in the third sector. Recent projects include working with Hartlepool and East Durham Mind to co-design and secure funding for a completely non-medicalised mental health and wellbeing initiative, maximising the skills and experience of peers and those with lived experience and using mutual aid models to grow capacity through COVID-19. In other work, she has been challenging the current support systems for differently abled young people leaving care and been central to designing a new living and learning centre offering person-centred, trauma-informed support toward independence, and is active in the creation of a new wellbeing strategy for small businesses across Durham, nurturing a more human approach to wellbeing that enables friends and colleagues to support one another rather than directing people to medical services. She is part of the movement for positive change and social justice, particularly in relation to 'mental health', finding answers in social and trauma-based understanding, peer support and mutual aid. Ruth believes in the importance of love, kindness, humanity and creativity.

Dr Brian Levitt

Dr Brian Levitt is a registered clinical and rehabilitation psychologist and a partner at Kaplan and Levitt Psychologists in Hamilton, Ontario. He works with people who have experienced trauma and loss, many of whom are also struggling with chronic pain. Person-centred theory and applications are an abiding passion, and he has explored these in all aspects of his work across a wide variety of settings. Brian has edited two books with PCCS Books: *Embracing Non-Directivity* and *Reflections on Human Potential.* His most recent book, also available through PCCS Books, is *Questioning Psychology: beyond theory and control,* in which he addresses what gets in the way of more fully understanding other people in all aspects of assessment and treatment in psychology.

Jo McFarlane

Jo McFarlane is a survivor of the psychiatric system who now writes, teaches and performs, using her personal experience to influence the reform of health and social care. She has written several books, as well as themed poetry collections, essays and memoirs, and has presented at more than 300 events across the UK, including recitals at the Scottish Parliament. She has been described as the 'poet laureate of recovery' and believes passionately in the power of love, hope and creativity to transform our lives for good.

James Moore

James Moore has experienced the psychiatric system and psychiatric drugs first-hand, following a stress-related breakdown. Believing himself to be fundamentally broken, he spent many years on psychiatric drugs before awakening to the reality that psychiatry has few answers for human difficulties. James produces and hosts the Mad in America podcast, in which he interviews experts and those with lived experience to challenge some common misconceptions about psychiatry, psychiatric drugs and the bio-medical model.

Matthew Morris

Matthew Morris is the Director of Development for Your Life Our Help (YLOH) and The Mavam Group. He has been working with people experiencing emotional distress since 1982, when he went to work at a Mind drop-in centre in Northampton. Matthew trained as a mental health nurse in Ipswich and qualified in 1990. He has worked in the NHS, the voluntary sector and now as part of an independent organisation. All of his working life, he has been involved in developing new teams and services, trying to create compassionate alternatives to the medical perspective.

Jacky Power

Jacky Power is a recovering human, mother, therapist, and spoken-word artist. She has an MSc in addiction psychology and counselling and specialises in social media addiction. Her writing has appeared in *Om Yoga* magazine, the Riza Press's 'The Uncertain Creative' COVID-19 support platform, the *For Women Who Roar* storytelling movement and various poetry anthologies. In 2019, she wrote and performed her own one-woman show called *Light in Life's Shadows*, which was about embracing the messiness of being human. If you spend more than five minutes with her, it is highly likely that you will be subjected to one of her poems. You have been warned.

Dolly Sen

As a child, Dolly Sen played an alien in *The Empire Strikes Back*. She knew then she would never know normal life. Dolly is an award-winning writer, artist, performer and filmmaker, which has taken her up a tree in Regent's Park, to California's Death Row, to the Barbican, Tower Bridge, and up a ladder to screw a light bulb into the sky. None of this would have happened if she had believed diagnosis and psychiatry define her. She has had 10 books published, been nominated twice for a Dadafest Literary Award (2006 and 2007) and won several awards for her poetry. Her subversive blogs around art, disability and humour have a huge international following. Since 2004, she has exhibited and performed internationally.

Clare Shaw

Clare Shaw has three collections published with Bloodaxe: *Straight Ahead* (2006), which attracted a Forward Prize Highly Commended for Best Single Poem; *Head On* (2012), which is, according to the *Times Literary Supplement*, 'fierce... memorable and visceral', and *Flood* (2018). Her forthcoming fourth collection was awarded a Northern Writer's Award in 2018. Clare was born in Burnley in 1972 and her poetry finds its roots in place and an uncompromising voice. Often addressing political and personal conflict, it is fuelled by a strong conviction in the transformative and redemptive power of language. Clare is an Associate Fellow with the Royal Literary Fund and a regular tutor for the Poetry School, the Wordsworth Trust, The National Writer's Centre of Wales and the Arvon Foundation. She is also a mental health trainer, activist and author. Recent publications include *Otis Doesn't Scratch: talking to young children about self-injury* (PCCS Books, 2015), and *Our Encounters with Self-Harm*, as co-editor (PCCS Books, 2013).

Mitzy Sky

Mitzy Sky shares her journey through writing, spoken-word-storytelling, and videography. She's consciously unlearning messages that she unconsciously learned that hindered her from living wholeheartedly. She is a contributor in the anthology *Imagining Monsters*. Her writing has been published on the Good Men Project, Mad in America and Inner-City News websites. She contributes to the Advocacy Unlimited newsletter, where she works in advocacy and education and developed the Compassionate Activism program. She is the creator of the Beyond the Story© project and Blogger/Vlogger at www.mitzysky.com

Erin Stevens

Erin Stevens is a counsellor/psychotherapist, writer and campaigner in private practice in Ilkley, West Yorkshire. She is a member of the Psychotherapists and Counsellors for Social Responsibility steering group, as well as a prominent campaigner on issues of social justice in counselling and psychotherapy. Outside of counselling, Erin enjoys writing rhyming verse, attending poetry groups and live performance.

Dr Jessica Taylor

Dr Jessica Taylor is the founder of VictimFocus, an international research, teaching and consultancy organisation with the sole aim of challenging the victim blaming and pathologisation of women and girls subjected to violence and abuse. She is a feminist psychologist with a PhD in forensic psychology, and a senior lecturer in forensic and criminal psychology. Jessica has written five books, including *Why Women Are Blamed for Everything*, and several chapters, articles and resources on the topics of child sexual abuse, rape, victim blaming, pathologisation of women, women bringing up babies from rape and global misogyny. She developed a free online course for survivors of sexual violence that was accessed by more than 20,000 people in its first eight months. Her VictimFocus blog has more than one million readers per year.

Joelle Taylor

Joelle Taylor is an award-winning poet, playwright, author and editor who has recently completed touring Europe, Australia, Brazil and South East Asia with her latest collection, *Songs My Enemy Taught Me*. She is widely anthologised, the author of three full poetry collections and three plays and is currently completing her debut book of short stories, *The Night Alphabet*. She has featured on radio and television, and founded SLAMbassadors in 2001, the UK's national youth slam championships, remaining its Artistic Director until 2018. Joelle's work is taught as part of the English GCSE syllabus, and she has received a Change Maker Award and a Fellowship of the RSA, as well as being longlisted for the Jerwood Compton Poetry Fellowships. She is the host and co-curator of Out-Spoken, the UK's Centre's premier poetry and music club, currently resident at the Southbank Centre Purcell Room.

Dr Karen Treisman

Dr Karen Treisman is a clinical psychologist, trainer, international speaker, and expert witness specialising in trauma. She is also an organisational consultant and supports organisations on their trauma-informed journey. Karen is a bestselling author and has written 10 books and produced four sets of therapeutic card decks, including *A Therapeutic Treasure Box for Working with Children and Adolescents with Developmental Trauma*, *Cleo the Crocodile Activity Book for Children who are Afraid to Get Close*, and *A Treasure Box for Creating Trauma-Informed Organizations*. Karen is also the founder and director of Safe Hands and Thinking Minds training and consultancy services. www.safehandsthinkingminds.co.uk

T.O. Walker

T.O Walker has worked in mental health on and off for 17 years. She has also used mental health services on and off for 22 years. She has had different diagnoses assigned or suggested to her but has found it much more useful and empowering to frame any struggles in terms of the context of her life. T.O. Walker is an author and illustrator. She has written a number of articles about mental health and illustrated *Otis Doesn't Scratch* (PCCS Books, 2015), a children's book about self-harm. More recently, she has written and illustrated a book based on her own experiences of trauma and dissociation in the context of sexual violence, *Not My Shame* (Jessica Kingsley Publishers, 2017).

Jo Watson (editor and contributor)

Jo Watson is a psychotherapist, trainer, speaker and activist. Her activism is motivated by a belief that emotional distress is caused by what is experienced and largely rooted in social factors. Jo founded the Facebook group 'Drop The Disorder!' in September 2016. She is part of the madintheuk.com team and editor of *Drop the Disorder! Challenging the culture of psychiatric diagnosis* (PCCS Books, 2019). Jo is the organiser of the AD4E events adisorder4everyone.com and can be found on Twitter @dropthedisorder

Jen Yates

Jenny is a budding poet, having dipped her toe into the creative waters, using her poetry to help explore past painful traumas and early parental bereavement. Following her own trauma therapy journey, Jenny started training as a humanistic counsellor in 2012. In her current private practice, based in Warwickshire, she works with a trauma-informed approach to allow clients safe exploration while offering a narrative to their suffering. Jenny is also the Wordpress content editor for the AD4E website (adisorder4everyone.com) and is a contributor at the Drop the Disorder! poetry events. www.counsellingwarwickshire.com

Drop The Disorder! Challenging the culture of psychiatric diagnosis

Edited by Jo Watson (2019)
pp. 270

ISBN – paperback 978 1 910919 46 0
        epub 978 1 910919 50 7
www.pccs-books.co.uk/products/drop-the-disorder

In October 2016 Jo Watson hosted the very first 'A Disorder for Everyone!' event in Birmingham, with psychologist Dr Lucy Johnstone, to explore (and explode) the culture of psychiatric diagnosis in mental health. To provide a space to continue the debate after the event, Jo also set up the now hugely popular and active Facebook group 'Drop the Disorder!'.

Since then, they have delivered events in towns and cities across the UK, bringing together activists, survivors and professionals to debate psychiatric diagnosis. How and why does psychiatric diagnosis hold such power? What harm it can do? What are the alternatives to diagnosis, and how it can be positively challenged?

This book takes the themes, energy and passions of the AD4E events – bringing together many of the event speakers with others who have stories to tell and messages to share in the struggle to challenge diagnosis.

This is an essential book for everyone of us who looks beyond the labels.

'Challenging, insightful and often controversial… a truly innovative and valuable book that functions both as a learning resource and an ardent call to arms.'
Dr Eleanor Longden, Psychosis Research Unit, Greater Manchester Mental Health NHS Foundation Trust